QUITO

BEN WESTWOOD

Contents

History 10
Climate 10
Orientation. 10
Safety 12
Planning Your Time 12

Sights 13
Old Town 13
North and East of Plaza Grande 19
Above Old Town. 21
Between Old Town and New Town 21
New Town 23
North of New Town. 23

Entertainment
and Events 27
Nightclubs and Discos 27
Bars, Pubs, And Cafés 28
Theaters and Concerts 30

Shopping 31
Crafts and Galleries. 31
Books 32
Magazines and Newspapers 32
Sporting Equipment 32
Jewelry and Accessories 32
Markets 32

Sports and Recreation 33
Climbing and Mountaineering 33
Biking. 34
Rafting and Kayaking 34
Horseback Riding 34
Spectator Sports 34
City Tours 34

Accommodations 36

Food 40

Information and Services ... 46

Visitor Information ... 46
Visas ... 46
Embassies and Consulates ... 46
Maps ... 46
Post Offices and Couriers ... 47
Telecommunications ... 47
Money ... 47
Health ... 48
Other Services ... 48

Getting There and Around ... 49

Getting There and Away ... 49
Getting Around ... 52

Vicinity of Quito ... 55

Calderón ... 55

Guayllabamba and Vicinity ... 55
Mitad del Mundo ... 55
The Pichinchas ... 59
Mindo ... 60
Maquipucuna Biological Reserve ... 65
Yanacocha ... 65
Tandayapa Lodge ... 65
Bellavista Cloud Forest Reserve ... 66
Hostería San Jorge ... 66
Sangolquí ... 67
Pasochoa Protected Forest ... 67

Quito

Highlights

© AVALON TRAVEL

★ **La Compañía:** The epitome of gaudy golden grandeur, this extravagant chapel is the most dazzling of all Quito's many beautiful colonial churches (page 16).

★ **La Basílica del Voto Nacional:** The tallest church in Ecuador with its armadillo gargoyles is a striking sight, and even more spectacular are the views from its spires over Old Town (page 20).

★ **Casa de la Cultura:** From Valdivia figurines to giant *bahía* statues and a majestic Inca sun mask, this is easily Ecuador's best museum (page 22).

★ **Capilla del Hombre:** Oswaldo Guayasamín's final work, the Chapel of Man, is an awe-inspiring and humbling tribute to the indigenous peoples of the Americas (page 26).

★ **Mitad del Mundo and Museo de Sitio Intiñan:** Take the obligatory photo with a foot in each hemisphere (supposedly), then test out the real Equator a few hundred meters away at nearby Museo de Sitio Intiñan (pages 55 and 57).

★ **Mindo:** This sleepy town, nestled in the cloud forest, teems with toucans, hummingbirds, quetzals, and butterflies. Adrenaline seekers can fly across the forest canopy on zip-lines or plunge down the river rapids (page 60).

Ecuador's capital is a city that scales many heights, not least in terms of elevation. The second-highest capital in the world after Bolivia's La Paz, Quito sits at 2,850 meters above sea level in a valley hemmed in by mountains, including the twin peaks of Volcán Pichincha. Quito's dramatic geographical position has led to its long thin shape: spread out over 50 kilometers long, but just eight kilometers wide.

Quito (pop. 1.6 million) is an intriguing mix of old and new: colonial squares and concrete office blocks, traditional markets and modern malls, indigenous artisans and fashion-conscious professionals—and this diversity allows visitors to have the best of both worlds. The *centro histórico* (historic center) delivers a delightful trip back in time to the colonial era with narrow cobbled streets, elegant plazas, and spectacular churches. New Town, on the other hand, looks firmly forward and is so cosmopolitan that parts of it are nicknamed *gringolandia*. With a vibrant cultural scene, great nightlife, a vast array of hotels, travel agencies, and the country's best range of restaurants, it's no surprise that Ecuador's political capital is also its tourism hub.

Much of the population of Ecuador's second-largest city lives in *barrios* (neighborhoods) or shantytowns, either up the slopes of the mountains or spread north and south of the city center. The people themselves are historically more conservative than in the rest of Ecuador; the capital has always clung to traditional, conservative values, in contrast to the outward-looking merchants of Guayaquil. However, a new generation, a large student population, and modern businesses have all injected a healthy dose of open-mindedness. Most importantly, visitors will find Quiteños helpful, welcoming, and justifiably proud of their city.

Quito's residents have plenty to be proud of: In 1978 it was the first city in the world to receive World Heritage Site status from UNESCO. Although there have been problems with upkeep, in recent years a multimillion-dollar regeneration program has left the city in better shape than ever. A new feeling of

Quito

© AVALON TRAVEL

0 0.5 mi
0 0.5 km

SEE "OLD TOWN QUITO" MAP

SEE "NEW TOWN QUITO" MAP

TELEFÉRICO

OCCIDENTAL/ SUCRE

BAHÍA DE CARÁQUEZ

El Panecillo

24 DE MAYO

LA COMPAÑÍA

GUAYAQUIL

Cumandá

Recoleta

MALDONADO

Santo Domingo

Cumandá Urban Park

PICHINCHA

Marin

Plaza del Teatro

Santa Prisca

LA BASÍLICA DEL VOTO NACIONAL

PALACIO LEGISLATIVO

Consejo Provincial

La Alameda

Parque La Alameda

COLOMBIA

TAROUÍ

El Ejido

Marin Central

MOSAICO

NUCANCHI PEÑA

UNIVERSITARIA

UNIVERSIDAD CENTRAL

LA GASCA

Seminario Mayor

AMERICA

Espejo

Perez Guerrero

POST OFFICE

10 DE AGOSTO

ELOY

ORELLANA

POST OFFICE

AMAZONAS

CAFELIBRO

COLON

Parque

PATRIA

CASA DE LA CULTURA

12 DE OCTUBRE

HOSTAL L'AUBERGE INN

INSTITUTO GEOGRÁFICO MILITAR

COLISEO RUMIÑAHUI

ITCHIMBIA PARK AND CULTURAL CENTER

LIBERTADOR

EL TREBOL

SIMÓN

BOLÍVAR

GRAL

LADRÓN

DE

GUEVARA

CINE OCHO Y MEDIA

HOTEL QUITO

IGLESIA GUAPULO

Guapulo

RUMIÑAHUI

Rio Machangara

To Trolé Estación Sur, El Recreo, and Moran Valverde

AVE CUMANDA

To Machachi, Latacunga and South

To Los Chillos

.... TROLÉ LINE
—·—·— ECOVIA LINE
■ TROLÉ/METROBUS
● ECOVIA STOP
— — METROBUS

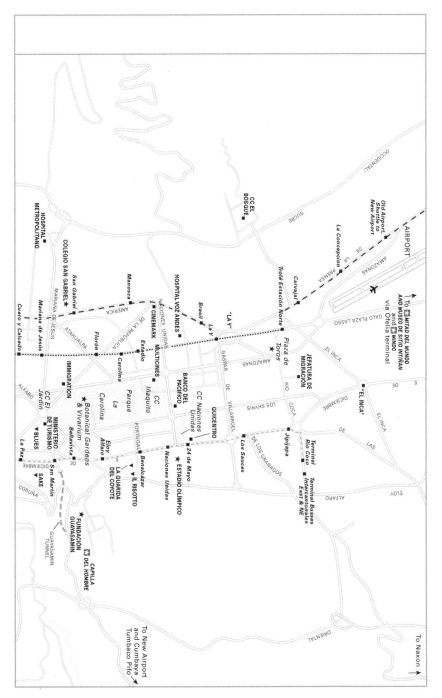

cleanliness and security pervades Old Town, with an increased police presence and a burgeoning cultural and nightlife scene. Interior patios have been tastefully renovated, and street artists have replaced beggars and hawkers. New Town is also increasingly well kept, although it has some way to go to solve its security problems.

HISTORY

According to a pre-Inca legend, the city of Quito was founded by Quitumbe, son of the god Quitu, in honor of his father. The valley that would eventually cradle Ecuador's capital was originally occupied by the Quitu people, who united with the Cara from the north to form the Shyris nation around AD 1300. In 1487 the Incas took over and turned the city into an important nexus of their northern empire, known as the Quitosuyo. Within 100 years the empire fell to infighting, leaving room for the newly arrived Spanish to start almost from scratch.

The city of San Francisco de Quito was founded by Sebastián de Benalcázar on December 6, 1534, and named in honor of fellow conquistador Francisco Pizarro. Benalcázar quickly set about appointing government officials, distributing land to his men, and constructing churches. Originally, Quito consisted only of the present-day section known as Old Town, bounded by the Plaza de San Blas to the north, the Pichinchas to the west, and the Machangara ravine to the east. An art school was founded in 1535 and helped the city become a center of religious art during the colonial period, with its own style, the Quito School.

Since its founding, Quito has been an administrative rather than a manufacturing center. A population boom in the mid-20th century, aided by the discovery of oil, brought thousands of immigrants who spread their homes and businesses into today's New Town, as well as farther south of Old Town and west up the slopes of Pichincha. By the mid-1980s, these makeshift *suburbios* housed as much as 15 percent of the city's population and had acquired most of the services that the older areas took for granted. An earthquake in 1987 damaged numerous structures and left others in ruins, and the eruption of Guagua Pichincha in 1999 showered Quito in ash but otherwise left the city unscathed. Today, the city is officially home to about 1.6 million residents, but the real number is likely higher.

CLIMATE

Quito is famed for its springlike climate, and most of the year daytime temperatures fluctuate 10-21°C. Mornings tend to be chilly, but it can heat up considerably around midday, and temperatures drop quickly on rainy afternoons and in the evenings. Locals say that the city can experience all four seasons in a single day, and that isn't far off the mark. The dry season lasts June-September, with July-August seeing the least precipitation. This is also the warmest time of year. A shortened dry season runs December-January, which is also the coldest time of year. The most rain falls February-April and, to a lesser extent, October-November. Afternoons tend to be rainier, so sightseeing early is a good idea.

More of a consideration than the weather is the elevation, which will leave you breathless and light-headed for a couple of days. Dizzy spells, headaches, and fatigue can also occur. It is best not to overexert yourself and to minimize caffeine and alcohol in favor of plenty of water and light food. After two or three days, you'll be used to the elevation.

ORIENTATION

Quito extends over 50 kilometers north-south, and about eight kilometers across. Luckily for first-time visitors, the capital is easily divided into zones: one for historical sights (Old Town); one for visitor services, restaurants, and accommodations (New Town); and then everything else. The city's long, narrow geography makes it quite easy to get around.

A new system of street numbers was implemented in Quito in 2000, with letters prefixing the normal hyphenated numbers (e.g., "Foch E4-132"). Most addresses also give the nearest cross street, so the full address would be "Foch E4-132 y Cordero."

Old Town

Quito's historical heart sits at the northern flank of El Panecillo (Little Bread Loaf) hill, whose statue of the Virgin is visible from most of the neighborhood. This area, also called Quito Colonial or *centro histórico* (historic center), is roughly bordered by 24 de Mayo to the south and Parque La Alameda to the north. Most of the sights are situated within a few blocks of the central Plaza de la Independencia, the original core of the city.

Steep, narrow streets characterize this part of Quito, and cars barely fit in lanes designed for horse and foot traffic. Wrought-iron balconies hang over ground-level storefronts selling household wares, clothing, and shoes.

Most visitors come for the outstanding churches, convents, museums, and plazas that are key to Quito's status as a UNESCO World Heritage Site. Other visitors are content to wander the cobbled streets that evoke Ecuador's colonial past.

There are many wonderful viewpoints to take in Old Town's impressive skyline—from the gothic spires of the Basílica to the top of El Panecillo or the green spaces of Parque Itchimbía.

New Town

Northeast of Old Town, Parque La Alameda and El Ejido form a buffer between past and present. New Town is a world away from the colonial cobbled streets of the historic center. The **Mariscal Sucre** area is the hub and aptly nicknamed *gringolandia* for its abundance of hotels, restaurants, tour operators, shops, Internet cafés, bars, and discos. This area, enclosed by Avenidas Patria, Orellana, 10 de Agosto, and 12 de Octubre, is alive with backpackers and also doubles as the city's main area for nightlife, heaving with partiers on weekends. North and east of La Mariscal are quieter neighborhoods such as La Floresta and González Suárez, as well as Quito's largest park, Parque Carolina. To the east, high above this park, is one of the highlights of the city, artist Oswaldo Guayasamín's famous work, La Capilla del Hombre (Chapel of Man).

Other Neighborhoods

The section of Quito north of New Town hosts much of the capital's industry and sparkles with shiny high-rises that house a large part of the city's businesses. These areas are of less interest to visitors. Modern shopping centers and chic restaurants cater to the middle and

Quito offers new discoveries around every corner.

upper classes that live in this area or in the fast-growing Valle Los Chillos and Tumbaco valleys, both to the east, which also have growing expat retirement communities. The dramatic beauty of the steep old neighborhood Guapulo spills down below Avenida 12 de Octubre and the lofty Hotel Quito. More residential neighborhoods occupy the lower slopes of Pichincha west and north of New Town.

SAFETY

Unfortunately, this most dramatic and historic of South American cities is not without its problems. Quito has rising crime rates, and although you shouldn't be alarmed, bear in mind that there is more crime against visitors here than in any other region of Ecuador. The high concentration of foreigners sadly has led to an increased number of criminals targeting them, so you must take precautions.

One of the diciest areas is the visitor-filled Mariscal Sucre neighborhood of New Town, sometimes simply called "La Mariscal." Increased police presence has recently improved the situation, but the neighborhood still harbors many thieves. Walking alone at night should be avoided; take a taxi to and from your hotel, preferably booked in advance. Don't get into an unmarked cab, and check for the orange license plate and registration number on the side of the vehicle, as "express kidnappings" (a robbery using a vehicle) have been reported.

Watch for pickpockets and bag-slashers on public transport and in Old Town in general. Pay particular attention in crowded areas and when exiting tourist spots like churches. Keep all bags and cameras in front of you, and don't leave your wallet in your back pocket. Don't go into any parks after dark. Beware of people "accidentally" spilling liquids on you and other diversionary tactics.

The trolleybus services (Trole, Ecovia, and Metrobus) are perhaps the worst for pickpockets, and it is guaranteed there will be several thieves on crowded services. It's simple: either keep your valuables well-hidden, or don't take them on the bus at all. Better yet, if you're going sightseeing, take a taxi. A ride from New Town to Old Town costs just $2-3.

The area around El Panecillo is not safe, so take a taxi to get there and back (the driver will usually wait for about $8 roundtrip). At the *teleférico* (cable car), assaults and muggings have been reported on the hike to Rucu Pichincha, although there are now police patrols on the weekend. Do not attempt this climb alone, and ideally don't take valuables.

PLANNING YOUR TIME

If the elevation doesn't make your head spin, the amount to see in Quito probably will. Quito can be a little overwhelming, and you simply can't see it all in a couple of days. You might even consider getting straight on a bus and going down in elevation to a quieter town (Otavalo, Mindo, or Baños) to get your bearings if you've just arrived in South America.

If you only have a couple of days here, spend one each in Old Town and New Town. Start at Plaza Grande and take in the cathedral, the presidential palace, La Compañía, and Plaza San Francisco before enjoying the views over the city at El Panecillo or La Basílica. In New Town, don't miss the Museo del Banco Central, the Guayasamín Museum, and the Capilla del Hombre. You may have time to visit the Equator at the Mitad del Mundo, or take an extra day to combine this with a hike to Pululahua for a little bird-watching and crater-viewing. The *teleférigo* (cable car) ride west of New Town offers the most spectacular views over the city at 4,000 meters.

Most visitors stay in New Town, mainly because there are so many visitor amenities. However, staying in Old Town is increasingly possible and offers a more authentic experience. It really depends on what you want: to hook up with kindred spirits for tours and to socialize at night, stay in New Town; for quieter and more cultural experiences, stay in one of the historic hotels in Old Town. Wherever you stay, it's only a short cab or bus ride between the two districts.

Sights

Quito's Old Town is what makes the city famous, containing a huge number of colonial churches and religious buildings set around elegant plazas. The walls and ceilings are decorated with elaborate paintings and sculptures, and altars are resplendent with gold leaf.

Flash photography is prohibited in most churches and historical museums to protect the fragile pigments of the religious paintings and statues. Keep in mind that opening hours fluctuate regularly; those provided here are the latest available. Several churches are currently undergoing extensive renovation work, but all are open.

OLD TOWN

Quito's Old Town is cleaner, safer, and a joy to wander around following a recent multimillion-dollar regeneration. Gone are the beggars and street vendors, replaced with police and horse-drawn carriages carting visitors around churches, which are beautifully lit at night. A system called Pico y Placa regulates traffic congestion by restricting the entry of certain license-plate numbers at peak hours. It has improved the traffic situation, although the narrow streets still struggle to accommodate Quito's cars. Cars are prohibited completely 9am-4pm Sunday, making it the most pleasant day for sightseeing.

The municipality of Quito has put together excellent guided maps to historic walks through Old Town, available at tourist offices. Even better are the multilingual tours given by municipal police from the tourist office.

Plaza Grande and Vicinity

This ornate 16th-century plaza is the political focal point of colonial Quito. Officially called the Plaza de la Independencia, it features a winged statue to independence atop a high pillar. The surrounding park is a popular gathering place with regular music, mime, and dance performances.

On the plaza's southwest side, the Catedral is actually the third to stand on this site (mass 6am-9am daily). Other visits are available through the museum located on Venezuela (tel. 2/257-0371, 9:30am-4pm Mon.-Fri., 10am-4pm Sun., $1.50). Hero of independence Antonio José de Sucre is buried here. Behind the main altar is the smaller altar of Nuestra Señora de Los Dolores, where, on August 6, 1875, president Gabriel García Moreno drew his last breath after being attacked with machetes outside the presidential palace. He is now buried here also, as is the country's first president, Juan José Flores.

Next door, formerly the main chapel of the cathedral, the Iglesia El Sagrario (7:30am-6pm Mon.-Sat., 7:30am-noon Sun.) was begun in 1657 and completed half a century later. The walls and ceiling of the short nave are painted to simulate marble—even the bare stone is speckled black-and-white. Impressive paintings and stained glass windows decorate the center cupola. Bernardo de Legarda, the most outstanding Quiteño sculptor of the 18th century, carved and gilded the baroque *mampara* (partition) inside the main doorway.

A long, arched atrium to the northwest lines the front of the handsome Palacio Presidencial (9am-noon and 3pm-5pm Tues.-Sun., free tours when the government is not in session), also known as El Carondelet. The ironwork on the balconies over the plaza, originally from the Tuileries Palace in Paris, was purchased just after the French Revolution. Current president Rafael Correa opened the doors of the palace to daily visitors in 2007, and it's worth making a line for the guided tours of the interior that leave every hour or so.

The Palacio Arzobispal (Archbishop's Palace) on the northeast side leads to a three-story indoor courtyard housing a number of small shops and eateries. Cobbled courtyards, thick whitewashed walls, and wooden

Old Town Quito

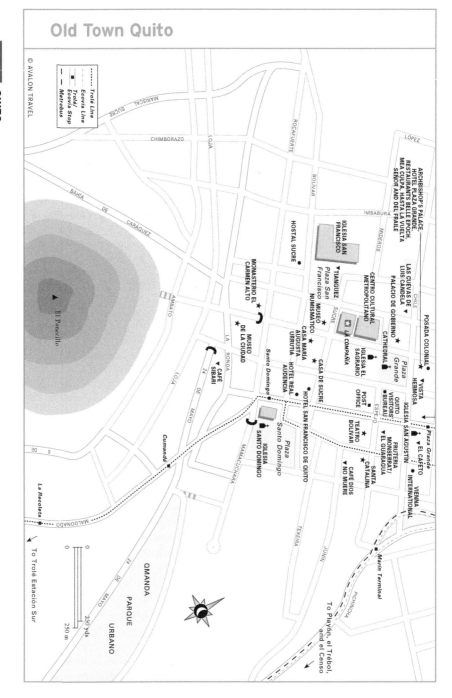

© AVALON TRAVEL

.... Trolé Line
— ■ — Ecovia Line
Trolé/
Ecovia Stop
— — Metrobus

MARISCAL SUCRE

CHIMBORAZO

ROCAFUERTE

LÓPEZ

BAHIA DE CARAQUEZ

LOJA

BOLIVAR

IMBABURA

ARCHBISHOP'S PALACE,
HOTEL PLAZA GRANDE,
RESTAURANTS BELLE EPOCH,
MEA CULPA, HASTA LA VUELTA
SEÑOR AND DEL FRAILE

CHILE

LAS CUEVAS DE
LUIS CANDELA

HOSTAL SUCRE

IGLESIA SAN
FRANCISCO

MIDEROS

MONASTERIO EL
CARMEN ALTO

TIANGUEZ

Plaza San
Francisco

CENTRO CULTURAL
METROPOLITANO
PALACIO DE GOBIERNO

POSADA COLONIAL

AMBATO

MUSEO
DE LA CIUDAD

SUCRE

MUSEO
NUMISMATICO

LA COMPAÑIA

CATHEDRAL

Plaza
Grande

VISTA
HERMOSA

EL CAFETO

El Panecillo

LA RONDA

CAFÉ
SIBARI

CASA MARIA
AUGUSTA
URRUTIA

CASA DE SUCRE

IGLESIA EL
SAGRARIO

QUITO
VISITORS
BUREAU

IGLESIA
SAN AGUSTIN

Plaza Grande

VIENNA
INTERNATIONAL

LOJA

24 DE MAYO

HOTEL REAL
AUDENCIA

POST
OFFICE

ESPEJO

FRUTERIA/
MONSERRATI,
EL GUARAGUA

6 DE

Santo Domingo

HOTEL SAN FRANCISCO DE QUITO

TEATRO
BOLIVAR

SANTA
CATALINA

Cumandá

IGLESIA
SANTO DOMINGO

Plaza
Santo Domingo

CAFE DIOS
NO MUERE

La Recoleta

MALDONADO

MAMACUCHARA

TEXEIRA

JUNIN

Marin Terminal

PICHINCHA

← To Trolé Estación Sur

0   250 yds
0   250 m

24 DE MAYO

OMANDA
PARQUE
URBANO

To Playón, el Trébol,
and el Censo

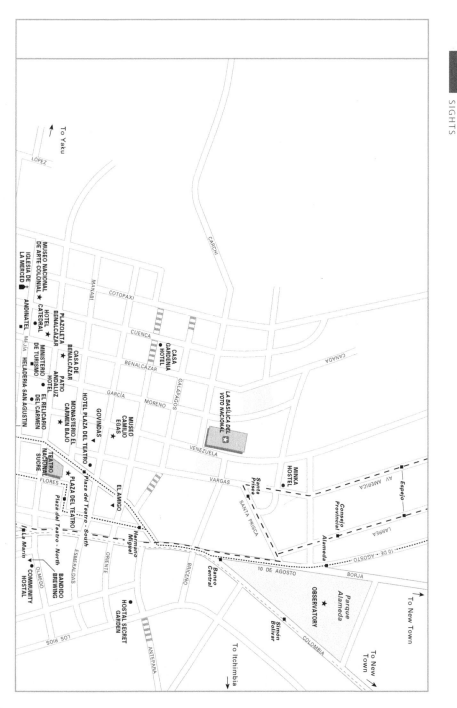

balconies make it worth a look. The plaza's colonial spell is broken only by the modern City Hall to the southeast. The church of La Concepción (10am-4pm Mon.-Fri., 10am-2pm Sat.-Sun.) stands at the corner of Chile and García Moreno. The attached convent is Quito's oldest, dating to 1577, and is closed to visitors.

At the corner of Benalcázar and Espejo, the Centro Cultural Metropolitano (tel. 2/295-0272, 9am-4:30pm daily) houses the collection of the Museo Alberto Mena Caamaño (tel. 2/258-4362, 9am-5pm Tues.-Sun., $1.50), which includes colonial and contemporary art and a set of wax figures depicting the death throes of patriots killed in 1810 by royalist troops. The cultural center also includes lecture rooms, the municipal library, and gallery space for temporary art exhibits.

★ La Compañía

La Compañía (9:30am-6:30pm Mon.-Thurs., 9:30am-5:30pm Fri., 9:30am-4pm Sat.,12:30pm-4pm Sun., $3) is one of the most beautiful churches in the Americas and certainly the most extravagant. Seven tons of gold supposedly ended up on the ceiling, walls, and altars of "Quito's Sistine Chapel," which was built by the wealthy Jesuit order

between 1605 and 1765. The church has been restored from the damage caused by the 1987 earthquake and a raging fire in 1996. It is a glorious example of human endeavor but at the same time borders on opulence gone mad.

Even the outside is overwhelming, crammed with full-size statues, busts, and sculpted hearts. The interior has eight side chapels, one of which houses the guitar and possessions of Quito's first saint, Santa Mariana de Jesús—her remains are under the main altar. Some of the more expensive relics, including a painting of the Virgin framed with gold and precious stones, are locked away in a bank vault between festivals. One of the more eye-catching objects in La Compañía is a painting depicting hell, where sinners—each labeled with one of the deadly sins—receive excruciating punishments.

Across Sucre from La Compañía is the Museo Numismático (tel. 2/258-9284, 9am-1pm and 2pm-5pm Tues.-Fri., 10am-1pm and 2pm-4pm Sat.-Sun., $1), which traces the history of Ecuador's various currencies, from shell currency to the adoption of the U.S. dollar. An inflation chart shows just how bad the economic situation used to be, before dollarization stabilized it in the last decade. Also housed here is the national

the Palacio Presidencial

music library, where there are often free concerts in the evenings. On the opposite side of García Moreno from the museum is the **Casa de María Augusta Urrutia** (García Moreno 760, between Sucre and Bolívar, tel. 2/258-0103, 10am-6pm Tues.-Sat., 9:30am-5:30pm Sun., $2), a wonderfully preserved 19th-century mansion. Doña María passed away in 1987, and her house is a virtual window on the past, with three inner patios and luxurious accoutrements from all over the globe, as well as a gallery of Victor Mideros's paintings.

Heading east on Sucre brings you to the **Casa de Sucre** (Venezuela 513 at Sucre), once home to Simón Bolívar's southern counterpart. The building has been preserved in its original state from the early 1800s, and the collection focuses on military history.

Plaza San Francisco and Vicinity

Turn right up the hill past La Compañía to one of Ecuador's most beautiful squares, **Plaza San Francisco.** This wide cobbled expanse is a highlight of the city, dominated by the wide facade of the **Iglesia San Francisco** (9am-5:30pm Mon.-Sat., 9am-1pm Sun.), the oldest colonial edifice in the city and the largest religious complex in South America. It was begun

on the site of an Inca royal house within weeks of the city's founding in 1534. The first wheat grown in Ecuador sprouted in one of its courtyards, and Atahualpa's children received their education in its school.

Two white spires flank a glowering stone facade, which sets the perfect mood for the interior. Inside, it's easy to imagine yourself in the 16th century, with the musty odor drifting up from the creaking wooden floorboards. Thick encrustations of gold cover almost every surface, and seeing the carved roof alone is worth a visit. Notice how many of the design motifs come from indigenous cultures, including the smiling and frowning faces of sun gods, repeated several times, and harvest symbols of flowers and fruit. At the time of this writing, the altar of the church was still undergoing a long and painstaking multiple-year restoration. Don't miss the choir rooms upstairs at the back of the church, adorned by statues of monks and the original wooden ceilings (enter through the museum).

To the right of the main entrance, the **Museo Fray Pedro Gocial** (tel. 2/228/1124, 9am-5:30pm Mon.-Sat., 9am-12:30pm Sun., $2) houses one of the finest collections of colonial art in Quito, dating from the 16th-19th centuries. Guided tours are included

La Compañía

in English, Spanish, and French. A highlight is the seven-meter-high portrait of the Franciscan family tree on the stairs leading up to the choir room. On the other side, the Capilla de Catuña (8am-noon and 3pm-6pm daily) also has colonial art on display. The story goes that this chapel was constructed by an indigenous man named Catuña who promised to have it completed in a certain amount of time. When it became obvious that he wasn't going to come close to his deadline, he offered his soul to the devil in exchange for help getting the job done. Catuña finished but had a sudden change of heart, begging the Virgin Mary to save him from his hasty agreement. Sure enough, a foundation stone was discovered missing during the inauguration, negating his deal with the devil.

The Tianguez café and gift shop downstairs is a great place to overlook the plaza with a coffee and a snack.

Plaza Santo Domingo and Vicinity

Down the hill southeast of Plaza San Francisco is the elegant Plaza Santo Domingo. A statue of Sucre pointing to the site of his victory on the slopes of Pichincha decorates the square. Crowds often surround performance artists in front of the Iglesia Santo Domingo (9am-5pm Mon.-Fri., 9am-1pm Sun.), which was begun in 1581 and finished in 1650. Four clock faces and an off-center tower decorate the stone facade. Despite the stained glass behind the altar, the decoration, much of which was completed in the 19th century, is a little muddled, although the baroque filigree of the Chapel of the Rosary to one side is stunning. The attached Museo Fray Pedro Bedon (tel. 2/228-0518, 9am-4:30pm Mon.-Fri., 9am-2pm Sat., $1) has obligatory tour guides to take you through the reserved chapels.

Nearby is one of the best-preserved colonial streets in Old Town. Also called Calle Juan de Díos Morales, La Ronda was nicknamed for the evening serenades (*rondas*) that once floated through its winding path. The narrow lane is lined with painted balconies, shops, tiny art galleries, and cafés. It's reached most easily via Guayaquil, sloping down from the Plaza Santo Domingo. This used to be a dangerous area, but an extensive regeneration has left it safe and one of the most popular evening haunts for Quiteños and visitors to soak up the atmosphere with a drink and some traditional music. It is well guarded and completely a pedestrian-only zone.

Plaza San Francisco

collection includes Inca burials, photographs, clothing, religious and scientific artifacts, scale models of the city at different periods, and a large painting depicting Francisco de Orellana's descent of the Amazon. Tours in English, French, Italian, and German can be arranged for an extra charge.

The Monasterio El Carmen Alto, opposite the museum at Rocafuerte and García Moreno, was the home of Santa Mariana de Jesús from 1618 to 1645. Abandoned children were once passed through a small window in the patio to be raised by the nuns. A small adjacent allows visitors to purchase cookies, chocolate, honey, creams, and herbs (9am-11am and 3pm-5pm Mon.-Fri.). The church is only open for 7am mass. The Arco de la Reina (Queen's Arch) over García Moreno marks the original southern entrance to Quito's center and once sheltered worshippers from the rain.

NORTH AND EAST OF PLAZA GRANDE
Iglesia de la Merced and Vicinity

The entrance to one of Quito's most modern churches, Iglesia de la Merced (8am-noon and 2pm-4pm Mon.-Fri.), completed in 1742, is on Chile, just up from the corner of Cuenca. The 47-meter tower houses the largest bell in town. Enter the high-vaulted nave, decorated with white stucco on a pink background, from the Plaza. The church is dedicated to Our Lady of Mercy, whose statue inside is said to have saved the city from an eruption of Pichincha in 1575. To the left of the altar is the entrance to the Monasterio de la Merced, housing Quito's oldest clock, built in London in 1817; a new clock face was recently installed. There are many paintings by Victor Mideros depicting the catastrophes of 1575.

Across Mejía is the Museo Nacional de Arte Colonial (Cuenca and Mejía, tel. 2/228-2297, 9am-5pm Tues.-Fri., 10am-2pm Sat., $2), home to Quito's finest collection of colonial art. Works by renowned artists Miáel de Santiago, Caspicara, and Bernardo de Legarda

Plaza Santo Domingo

Directly below La Ronda is the newest development in the area's makeover, the urban park Qmandá (S2 Av. 24 de Mayo, tel. 2/257-3645, 7am-8pm daily, $1-5), a masterpiece of urban renewal. Located in a refurbished former bus station, the park has seven swimming pools, a gym, a soccer field, a volleyball court, ping pong tables, and weekly classes. The three-story complex acts as a cultural center as well. Art and photography exhibits are displayed on the lower levels alongside a sprawling satellite map of Ecuador with a 3-D sculpture of Quito.

Museo de la Ciudad and Monasterio El Carmen Alto

Just up from La Ronda is Museo de la Ciudad (García Moreno and Rocafuerte, tel. 2/228-3879, 9:30am-5:30pm Tues.-Sun., $3). One of Old Town's best museums, it traces the history of the city from precolonial times to the beginning of the 20th century. It is set in the old Hospital San Juan de Díos, founded at the order of King Philip in 1565. The make up part of the collection, which has been extensively renovated.

A few blocks away, the colonial mansion and beautiful courtyard of Casa de Benalcázar (Olmedo 962 at Benalcázar, tel. 2/228-8102, 9am-1pm and 2pm-5pm Mon.-Fri., free) is worth a visit. It was built in 1534, the year of Quito's refounding.

★ La Basílica del Voto Nacional

Walk eight blocks northeast from Plaza Grande on Venezuela for the best view of Old Town from within its boundaries. Even though construction began in 1892, La Basílica del Voto Nacional (9am-5pm daily, $2) is still officially unfinished. However, its two imposing 115-meter towers make this the tallest church in Ecuador. Notice that the "gargoyles" are actually a menagerie of local animals, including armadillos. After appreciating the stained glass and powerful gilt statues in the nave, ride the elevator up to take in the fantastic views. Climb up unnerving stairs and metal ladders to the roof on the northern steeple or, even more unnerving, a higher point on the east tower. Tread carefully.

Iglesia San Agustín and Vicinity

East of Plaza Grande, the Iglesia San Agustín (Chile and Guayaquil, 7am-noon and 1pm-5pm Mon.-Fri., 8am-noon Sat.-Sun.) contains no surface left unpainted, including the likenesses of saints that line the arches against a pastel background. A black Christ occupies a side altar. The adjoining Convento y Museo de San Agustín (Chile and Flores, tel. 2/295-5525, 9am-12:30pm and 2:30pm-5pm Mon.-Fri., 9am-1pm Sat., $1) features a feast of colonial artwork on the walls and surrounds a palm-filled cloister. Ecuador's declaration of independence was signed in the *sala capitular* on August 10, 1809; don't miss the incredible carved benches and altar. Many of the heroes who battled for independence are buried in the crypt.

the narrow street of La Ronda

Plaza del Teatro and Vicinity

This small plaza at Guayaquil and Manabí is surrounded by restored colonial buildings, including the Teatro Nacional Sucre, one of Quito's finest theaters. The gorgeous building, erected in 1878, also has a wonderful restaurant called Theatrum on the second floor above the lobby. The theater hosts frequent plays and concerts, including opera, jazz, ballet, and international traveling groups. Tucked in the far corner is the renovated Teatro Variedades, reborn as an elegant dinner theater. Next door is the popular Café Teatro.

Enter the Monasterio El Carmen Bajo (Venezuela between Olmedo and Manabí, 8:30am-noon and 3:30pm-5pm Mon.-Fri., free) through huge wooden doors that date to the 18th century. Whitewashed stone pillars support a two-story courtyard inside, surrounded by nuns' quarters and schoolrooms.

Teatro Bolívar

Scorched by a fire in 1999, only two years

after an extensive restoration, the opulent Teatro Bolívar (Pasaje Espejo 847 y Guayaquil, tel. 2/258-3788, www.teatrobolivar.org) is being restored yet again. The 2,200-seat theater was built in 1933 by a pair of American theater architects, and it incorporates elements of art deco and Moorish styles. The theater is on World Monuments Watch's 100 Most Endangered Sites list and is currently open during restoration. Your ticket price will help fund the ongoing work, and you can make an additional donation.

Santa Catalina

The newly opened Convent Museo Santa Catalina (Espejo and Flores, tel. 2/228-4000, 8:30am-5pm Mon.-Fri., 8:30am-12:30pm Sat., $1.50) is housed with the church of the same name. The remains of assassinated president Gabriel García Moreno rested here secretly for many years before being buried under the cathedral. Many of his personal effects are on display, and his heart is buried in the private chapel. There is also a wide-ranging display of religious art and artifacts. A guided tour is included in the price and is recommended because the collection is spread among many rooms.

ABOVE OLD TOWN
El Panecillo

Old Town's skyline is dominated by a 30-meter statue of the Virgin of Quito on the hill at the southern end. The close-up view of the Virgin with a chained dragon at her feet is very impressive, and although she's nicknamed the "Bailarina" (Dancing Virgin), she's actually preparing to take flight. You can climb up inside the base (9am-4pm Mon.-Fri., 9am-5pm Sat.-Sun., $1) to an observation platform for a spectacular view of the city. The neighborhood on the way up is dangerous, so take a taxi and ask the driver to wait. The area at the top of the hill has security until 7pm. A taxi ride costs about $3-4 one-way, $8 round-trip including a short wait.

Itchimbía Park and Cultural Center

The old Santa Clara market building—imported from Hamburg in 1899 and brought to the highlands by mule, in sections—has been transported from Old Town and rebuilt in all its glass-and-metal glory on top of a hill to the east. The structure is now a cultural center (tel. 2/295-0272, ext. 137, 9am-5pm daily, $1) hosting occasional exhibitions, but the more common reason to come here is the view. The vicinity is more pleasant than El Panecillo, if not quite as spectacular, and not as hair-raising as climbing the Basílica. The center is surrounded by a 34-hectare park that is being reforested and laced with footpaths. It is beautifully lit up at night, and the views are great by day too. Just below on Samaniego is the restaurant Mosaico, along with several happening spots for drinks and elite elbow-rubbing that justify their prices every evening at sunset. A taxi from Old Town costs $3.

La Cima de la Libertad

In the foothills of Pichincha to the west of Old Town stands this military museum and monument to Sucre's decisive victory over the royalist forces at the Battle of Pichincha on May 24, 1822. At the Templo de la Patria, an expansive mosaic of the independence struggle by Eduardo Kingman competes with the view of the city and snowcapped volcanoes on clear days. The Museo de las Fuerzas Armadas (tel. 2/228-8733, 9am-5pm Mon.-Fri., 10am-4pm Sat.-Sun., $1) displays a modest collection of historical military tools and weapons as well as a scale model depicting the battle. Not many visitors make it up here; there are occasional buses, or take a taxi from Old Town (from $5).

BETWEEN OLD TOWN AND NEW TOWN
Parque la Alameda

Ornamental lakes and a monument to Simón Bolívar hold down opposite ends of this triangular park. In the center stands the oldest astronomical observatory in South

America, inaugurated in 1864 by then-president García Moreno. If you've visited observatories in North America and Europe, it may come up short, but it's still worth a visit. The beautiful old building also houses a museum (tel. 2/257-0765, 9am-noon and 2:30pm-5:30pm daily, $1) filled with books, photos, and antique astronomical tools, including a brass telescope that still works. Visitors can sometimes view the stars on clear nights; call ahead for a schedule and information on occasional astronomy lectures. Many of the large trees were planted in 1887, when the park began as a botanical garden.

Palacio Legislativo

Just north of Parque la Alameda at Gran Colombia and Montalvo, drop by when this arm of Ecuador's government is out to lunch and you can peek through the fence to see Oswaldo Guayasamín's infamous 1988 mural titled *Imagen de la Patria*. The huge work, depicting and protesting injustice in Latin America, caused a stir during its unveiling at a formal ceremony of ambassadors and dignitaries. An evil-looking face with a helmet labeled CIA caused the U.S. ambassador to storm out of the room. Copies of the mural are available in the Guayasamín Museum.

★ Casa de la Cultura

On the northern edge of Parque El Ejido, this curved glass building looks rather like a convention center, but don't let that dissuade you from visiting the best collection of museums in Ecuador. The Casa de la Cultura (tel. 2/222-3392, www.cce.org.ec, 9am-5pm Tues.-Fri., 10am-4pm Sat.-Sun., $2) was remodeled in 2005. The centerpiece of the complex is Museo del Banco Central, a world unto itself and easily Ecuador's most impressive museum. The collection includes more than 1,500 pieces of pre-Inca pottery, gold artifacts, and colonial and contemporary art, all labeled in English and Spanish.

The first hall is the massive Sala de Arqueología, which contains archaeology from Ecuador's long line of indigenous cultures: Figurines from the Valdivia, animal-shaped bottles from the Chorrera, one-meter-high statues known as *gigantes de la bahía* (bay giants), and Manteña thrones are just a few of the vast array of pieces.

A vault downstairs protects a dazzling collection of gold pieces: masks, breastplates, headdresses, and jewelry, many decorated with motifs of cats, serpents, and birds. The highlight is the majestic Inca sun mask, the symbol of the museum.

Upstairs is the Sala de Arte Colonial, which contains a massive 18th-century altar and a large collection of paintings and polychrome carvings from the Quito School. There are adjacent rooms dedicated to republican and contemporary art, the highlight being several paintings by renowned artist Oswaldo Guayasamín. The Casa also contains collections of furniture and musical instruments.

The Agora, a huge concert arena in the center of the building, hosts concerts (admission varies). There's also a *cine* showing art and cultural films most evenings.

The old building on 6 de Diciembre, facing the park, houses occasional exhibits and a bookshop that sells its own publications. Next door is the Teatro Prometeo, open for evening performances.

Parque El Ejido

Avenidas Patria, 6 de Diciembre, 10 de Agosto, and Tarquí form the wedge filled by Quito's most popular central park, Parque El Ejido. It's all that remains of the common grazing lands that stretched for more than 10 kilometers to the north. The park played its part in one of the most infamous moments in Ecuador's history when liberal president Eloy Alfaro's body was dragged here and burned following his assassination. These days, the most heated things get is during a game of *Ecuavolley* (the local version of volleyball) in the northwest corner of the park most evenings and weekends; a children's playground takes up the northeast corner. You can also often see people playing an Ecuadorian version of a French game of *boules*. On weekends, the area near the arch at Amazonas and Patria becomes an outdoor arts and crafts market; paintings line the sidewalk along Patria, and Otavaleños and other artists sell textiles, antiques, and jewelry.

NEW TOWN

New Town is where most visitors, particularly backpackers, stay in Quito and go out in the evenings. The commercial artery of this sector is Avenida Amazonas, and the busiest area lies just off the avenue in the blocks around Plaza Foch. Here you'll find all the visitor amenities: hotels, restaurants, bars, Internet cafés, banks, shops, and travel agencies. It's not nicknamed *gringolandia* for nothing, and the contrast with Old Town is striking; this sector has a decidedly international feel, which may or may not suit you. On the plus side, you can meet plenty of kindred spirits in the bars and cafés, and the nightlife is particularly raucous Thursday-Saturday. The biggest concentration of quality international cuisine in Ecuador is also here, and there are several 24-hour coffee shops for night owls. However, if you want to escape the hordes of foreign visitors and have a more authentic Andean experience, you may be tempted to spend your time elsewhere.

Museo Jacinto Jijón y Caamaño

The family of a prominent Ecuadorian archaeologist donated his private collection of colonial art and archaeological pieces to the Universidad Católica after his death. Now it's on display at the Museo Jacinto Jijón y Caamaño (tel. 2/299-1700, ext. 1242, 9am-4pm Mon.-Fri., $0.60), located within the university compound on the third floor of the main library building. Enter off 12 de Octubre near Carrión—ask the guard to point you in the right direction. Nearby in the Central Cultural block is the extensive Weilbauer collection.

Museo Amazónico

The small Abya Yala complex (12 de Octubre 1430 at Wilson, tel. 2/396-2800) contains a bookstore with the city's best selection of works on the indigenous cultures of Ecuador. Shops downstairs sell snacks, crafts, and natural medicines, while the second floor is taken up by the small but well-organized Museo Amazónico (8:30am-12:30pm and 2pm-5pm Mon.-Fri., $2). Guided tours are available in Spanish to take you past stuffed rainforest animals, stunning Cofán feather headdresses, and real Shuar *tsantsas* (shrunken heads). The pottery depicting lowland Kichwa gods, each with its accompanying myth, is particularly interesting, as are photos of oil exploration and its environmental impact.

Mindalae Ethnic Museum

Run by the Sinchi Sacha Foundation, which promotes indigenous cultures, fair trade, and responsible tourism, the Mindalae Ethnic Museum (Reina Victoria and La Niña, tel. 2/223-0609, 9am-4pm Mon.-Fri., 10am-4pm Sat., $3) has five floors with comprehensive collections of ethnic clothing, artifacts, and ceramics from all regions, plus a shop and a restaurant.

NORTH OF NEW TOWN
Parque La Carolina

If you want to escape the concrete of New Town without actually leaving the city, the nearest place to do so is Quito's largest park, Parque La Carolina, which stretches from the intersection of Orellana and Eloy Alfaro almost one kilometer east to Naciones Unidas. It's popular with early-morning joggers, and the *laguna* has two-person paddleboats for rent.

Natural history is the focus of the dusty Museo de las Ciencias Naturales (Rumipamba 341 at Los Shyris, tel. 2/244-9824, 8:30am-4:30pm Mon.-Fri., 10am-2pm Sat., $2), at the east end of the park. Here the Casa de la Cultura administers displays on zoology, botany, and geology, including a huge collection of dead spiders and an

New Town Quito

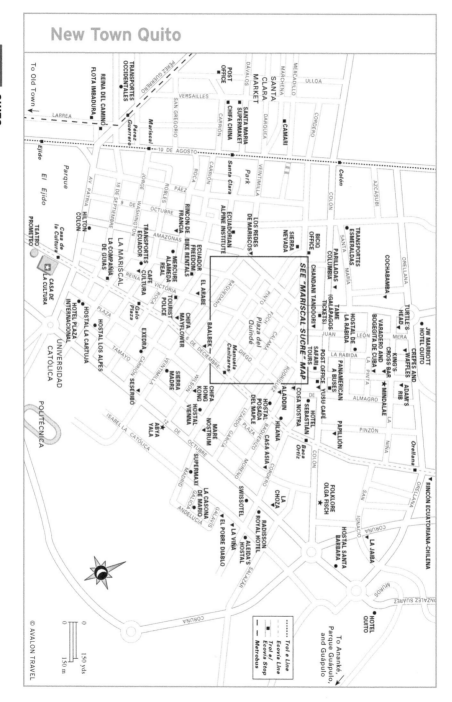

© AVALON TRAVEL

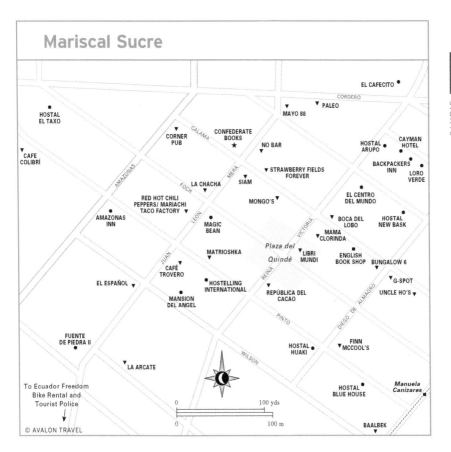

Mariscal Sucre

EL CAFECITO

CORDERO

PALEO

HOSTAL
EL TAXO

MAYO 88

CALAMA
CORNER
PUB

CONFEDERATE
BOOKS ★

NO BAR

HOSTAL
ARUPO

CAYMAN
HOTEL

CAFE
COLIBRÍ

BACKPACKERS
INN

LORO
VERDE

AMAZONAS

MERA

STRAWBERRY FIELDS
FOREVER

FOCH
LA CHACHA

SIAM

RED HOT CHILI
PEPPERS/ MARIACHI
TACO FACTORY

MONGO'S

EL CENTRO
DEL MUNDO

AMAZONAS
INN

LEON

MAGIC
BEAN

VICTORIA

BOCA DEL
LOBO

HOSTAL
NEW BASK

MAMA
CLORINDA

MATRIOSKA

Plaza del
Quindé

LIBRI
MUNDI

ENGLISH
BOOK SHOP

BUNGALOW 6

JUAN

CAFÉ
TROVERO

REINA

EL ESPAÑOL

HOSTELLING
INTERNATIONAL

REPÚBLICA DEL
CACAO

DIEGO DE ALMAGRO

G-SPOT

UNCLE HO'S

MANSION
DEL ANGEL

PINTO

FUENTE
DE PIEDRA II

WILSON

HOSTAL
HUAKI

FINN
MCCOOL'S

Manuela
Canizares

LA ARCATE

To Ecuador Freedom
Bike Rental and
Tourist Police

0   100 yds

0   100 m

HOSTAL
BLUE HOUSE

BAALBEK

© AVALON TRAVEL

anaconda skeleton. Fans of creepy-crawlies will enjoy the **Vivarium** (Amazonas 3008 at Rumipamba, tel. 2/227-1820, 9:30am-5:30pm Tues.-Sun., $2.50), with more than 100 live reptiles and amphibians. The collection includes poisonous and constrictor snakes from the Oriente. You can have your photo taken with a six-meter-long python ($3) if that appeals. If you're more into flora than fauna, visit the **Jardín Botánico** (between Ciencias Naturales and Shyris, 9am-4pm daily, $3), which showcases Ecuador's vast array of flora, including some 500 species of orchids in the greenhouses.

For a modern shopping experience, three large **shopping malls** surround the park: El Jardín (Avenida de La República and Amazonas), Iñaquito (Amazonas and Naciones Unidas), and Quicentro (Naciones Unidas and Avenida de Los Shyris).

Parque Carolina, like most of Quito's parks, is not safe after dark.

Museo Fundación Guayasamín

East of Parque Carolina, up a steep hill in the Bellavista neighborhood, the former home of Ecuador's most famous artist has been converted into the **Museo Fundación Guayasamín** (Bosmediano 543, tel. 2/244-6455, 10am-5pm Tues.-Sun., $3). Pre-Columbian figurines and pottery fill the first building, while Oswaldo Guayasamín's paintings and an impressive collection of colonial art wait farther on. Guayasamín's large-scale paintings are alternately tender and tortured but are always deeply emotive. The balcony outside has a café. In the gift shop, ask to see the many unique pieces of jewelry designed by the master himself. The artist is buried beneath the Tree of Life in the gardens of his house just above the museum.

To get to the museum, take a bus bound for Bellavista from Parque Carolina (marked "Batan-Colmena") or hail a taxi ($2).

★ Capilla del Hombre

You can't see everything in Quito, but whatever you do, don't miss Oswaldo Guayasamín's masterwork. Completed three years after his death in 1999 by the Guayasamín foundation, the Chapel of Man (Calvachi and Chavez, tel. 2/244-8492, www.capilladelhombre.com, 10am-5pm Tues.-Sun., $6) is dedicated to the struggles endured by the indigenous peoples of the Americas before and after the arrival of the Spanish.

Huge paintings fill the open two-story building, which is centered on a circular space beneath an unfinished dome mural portraying the millions of workers who died in the silver mines of Potosí, Bolivia. Other works cover topics both heartening and wrenching, from the tenderness of a mother and child's embrace in *La Ternura* to the gigantic *Bull and Condor,* symbolizing the struggle between Spanish and Andean identities. In the center of the ground floor burns an eternal flame. Guided tours are offered in English and Spanish.

Visitors receive a discount on entrance fees if they visit both the chapel and the Guayasamín museum in the same day, although this is only possible Tuesday-Friday. The chapel is a 10-minute walk up the hill from the museum.

Guápulo

Take the precipitous Camino de Orellana down the hill behind the Hotel Quito—or the footpath from the park and playground—to reach this hillside neighborhood. Although small compared to the city, this quaint neighborhood is quickly becoming the place to be, with new hotels and restaurants popping up at every turn. Narrow cobbled streets are lined with shops, cafés, and homes, including lavish walled-in residences favored by ambassadors, a world away from Quito's New Town. At the center is the 17th-century plaza fronting the beautiful Iglesia de Guápulo, built between 1644 and 1693 on the site of an even older convent. The sparkling church can be

Guayasamín's Capilla del Hombre

seen from far above and houses a collection of colonial art, including crucifixes and a pulpit carved by Juan Bautista Menacho in the early 18th century.

A fifteen-minute walk up the road behind the church and nestled in the hills above is Parque Guápulo (E35 Av. de los Conquistadores, 6am-6pm daily). Previously a wealthy banker's estate, the park has running paths, an exhibition area, and small lakes and gardens. It's also home to Educación Asistida con Caballos, a flourishing organization that provides interactive horse activities for people with disabilities.

Teleférigo (Cable Car)

Quito's most dizzying tourist attraction is the teleférigo (cable car) ride (tel. 2/225-0825, 10am-4pm Mon.-Fri., 9am-8pm Sat.-Sun., $9), which climbs up the slopes of Pichincha. Completed in 2005, it departs from above Avenida Occidental, where a tourist center with restaurants, a café, and a small theme park has been built. The 2.5-kilometer ride takes about 10 minutes. After a big rush of visitors in its first year, the teleférigo lost some of its popularity, but the breathtaking views over the city and the Andes from 4,050 meters make it worth the trip. It's busiest on the weekend, when there is also more security. From the top, you can hike three kilometers to Rucu Pichincha, but don't do this walk alone because robberies have been reported. Teleférigo shuttles run from Río Coca y 6 Diciembre (Ecovia) and Estación Norte (Trole).

Entertainment and Events

Quito has a thriving nightlife scene centered around Plaza Foch, Reina Victoria, and Calama in Mariscal Sucre. These blocks heave with locals and visitors Thursday, Friday, and Saturday evenings. Historically, things don't really get going until after 11pm, but a law now prohibits alcohol sales after midnight Monday-Thursday and after 2am Friday-Saturday. This has compelled young people to go out earlier, although many establishments stay open later regardless. Most of the dance clubs and discos include a small cover charge (usually $3-5), which includes a drink. Many bars have happy hours 5pm-8pm to bring in the crowds earlier, and several have ladies nights with free drinks before 10pm. After hours, there are a couple of cafés that stay open 24 hours, but late-night alcohol sales are officially banned. Most bars, discos, and even many restaurants are closed on Sundays.

As well as being the most popular nightlife spot, at night Mariscal Sucre is also the most risky area for foreign visitors. Walk just a couple of blocks away from the main drag and the police presence is replaced by groups of thieves looking for an opportunity. You can reduce the risk by taking a taxi to and from your hotel, even if it's only a few blocks away. Don't take valuables, credit cards, or more cash than necessary (you're unlikely to spend more than $30, unless it's a big celebration).

To avoid hassles while out and about, take a copy of your passport. Police have been known to randomly check for identification in bars and clubs and have also gone so far as to require a notarized copy. Check with the staff at your hotel to find out the most recent requirements.

NIGHTCLUBS AND DISCOS

By far the most popular spot in Mariscal is the American- and British-run Bungalow 6 (Calama and Almagro, tel. 2/254-7957, 8pm-midnight Weds.-Thurs., 8pm-2am Fri.-Sat., cover $5). Recently expanded to three floors, this friendly place is where Quito's college crowd mixes on the dance floor with backpackers. It gets very busy downstairs on the weekend after 11pm, but there's always a quieter spot upstairs for a drink. Ladies night is Wednesday.

Elsewhere, the discos in Mariscal are decidedly hit and miss. If you're looking for total mayhem, try out the meat market of No Bar (Calama and Juan León Mera, tel. 2/245-5145, 8pm-midnight Mon.-Thurs., 8pm-2am Fri.-Sat., cover $5). Somewhere among the gyrating bodies is a pool table.

One of the few late-night bars in Quito is Blues (República 476 at Pradera, tel. 2/246-0743, www.bluesestodo.com, 10pm-6am Thurs.-Sat., cover $7-15), spinning a mix of electronic and rock with international DJs and live rock bands on Thursdays to a style-conscious crowd.

BARS, PUBS, AND CAFÉS

Quito's sizable expat population from Europe and North America can't do without their draft beer, and a few decent pubs have been doing great business in the city for years. Perhaps the best ales can be found at the The Turtle's Head (La Niña 626 at Juan León Mera, tel. 2/265-5544, 4pm-midnight Mon.-Thurs., 4pm-2am Fri.-Sat.), a few blocks from the main drag. Even though the Scottish owner has moved on, the legacy of microbrew beers lives on. They also have pool, darts, and food.

One block from the center of the Mariscal scene, Irish-run Finn McCool's (Almagro N24-64 at Pinto, tel. 2/252-1780, www.irishpubquito.com, 11am-midnight Mon.-Thurs., 11am-2am Fri.-Sat.) has developed into the most popular expat pub, attracting a multinational crowd for pool, foosball, and streamed sporting events. Dirty Sanchez (Joaquin Pinto E7-38 y Reina Victoria 530 at Roca, tel. 2/255-1810, 5pm-midnight Mon.-Thurs., 5pm-2am Fri.-Sat.), has an eclectic, underground vibe with live music and DJs during the week and on weekends. The Dutch-owned Corner Pub (Amazonas and Calama, tel. 2/290-6608, 1pm-midnight Mon.-Thurs., 1pm-2am Fri.-Sat.) is a friendly bar that has quickly become popular with expats and visitors.

For a trip back to the 1960s, visit Beatles bar Strawberry Fields Forever (Calama and Juan León Mera, tel. 9/920-0454, 5pm-midnight Mon.-Thurs., 5pm-2am Fri.-Sat.), adorned with memorabilia, a menu of cocktails named after Beatles songs, and a Yellow Submarine-themed restroom. It attracts a creative Bohemian crowd and is a welcome break from the Mariscal madness.

Jazz and the occasional singer or poetry reader attracts an arty crowd to Café Libro (Leonidas Plaza and Wilson, tel. 2/223-4265, www.cafelibro.com, noon-2pm and 5pm-midnight Mon.-Sat.). Well-stocked bookshelves and photos of writers decorate this literary place. G-Spot (Diego de Almagro E8-10 y Calama, tel. 097/952-7439, 11am-midnight Mon.-Thurs., 11am-2am Fri.-Sat., 11am-6pm Sun.) is frequented by expats and travelers in search of sports broadcasts, tasty microbrews from Roches Brewery in Canoa, and good burgers and Mexican food. Recently renovated, the funky decor, a changing menu that includes items like different varieties of BBQ wings, and attentive staff make it the hip joint to rub elbows with locals most days of the week.

Elsewhere in Mariscal, there are plenty of attractive restaurants that double as great places for a drink. Standing out from the crowd is the colorful glass-encased Boca del Lobo (Calama 284 at Reina Victoria, tel. 2/223-4083, 5pm-midnight Mon.-Thurs., 5pm-2am Fri.-Sat.). Chic and stylish with rather surreal decor and an eclectic Mediterranean menu, it's a great place to indulge. Red Burger Society (Andalucia N24-234 y Cordero, tel. 2/604-0882, noon-midnight and 5pm Mon.-Sat., noon-5pm Sun.) is a chic restaurant with an impressive cocktail menu, generous happy hour specials, and reasonably priced gourmet burgers and appetizers.

Gay bars are harder to find and in a conservative culture, the Internet is probably the best source of information; www.quitogay.net has useful recommendations. The best-known are Bohemio (Baquedano and 6 de

Diciembre, tel. 2/221-4127, 10pm-3am Fri.-Sat.), also known as El Hueco, and **El Divino** (Foch E4-298 between Juan León Mera y Amazonas, tel. 8/441-6977, 8pm-midnight Wed.-Thurs., 8pm-2am Fri.-Sat.). Take a taxi to and from these bars.

There is a certain herd mentality to going out in Mariscal, and it's not for everyone. If you want a quieter evening, head to La Floresta, where ★ **El Pobre Diablo** (Isabel la Católica E12-06 at Galavis,tel. 2/222-5397, noon-3pm and 7pm-midnight Mon.-Thurs., 7pm-2am Fri.-Sat.) is still one of the best places for live music in Quito. Bands play a range of jazz, blues, and world music several times a week here, particularly on Wednesdays and Saturdays. The diverse cocktail menu, fusion food, and sophisticated crowd make for a great atmosphere. In the neighborhood of Guápulo is **Ananké** (Camino de Orellana 781, tel. 2/255-1421, 6pm-midnight Mon.-Sat.), a funky little spot with great views from both floors by day, and DJs and chill-out rooms upstairs by night. The pizzas are a specialty, as is the baked camembert starter.

At the end of Guapulo valley is **Cumbayá,** a sprawling developing suburb of Quito. It's home to the University of San Fransciso, many of the best international schools, and a newly constructed football-stadium-sized mall. Many new restaurants are springing up as the town grows. If venturing out of Quito proper for a subdued but joyful night out, check out **Bigoté** (Interoceanica y Diego de Robles, tel. 2/289-6422, 8am-8pm Mon.-Fri., 10am-4pm Sat.-Sun.), a small café catering to students and offering breakfast food, snacks, and sandwiches along with locally produced Guayusa tea and organic coffee. Or try **St. Andrew's Pub** (Av. Francisco de Orellana 640 y Manabí, tel. 02/289-0064, Mon.-Thurs. noon-midnight, Fri.-Sat. noon-2am, Sun. noon-6pm), an authentic Scottish pub with steaks, bangers and mash, hearty sandwiches, and tasty microbrews on tap. During the day, St. Andrew's has a two-for-one main course until 4pm. Also in Cumbayá, **Cats** (Lizardo García N537 y Diego de Almagro, tel. 2/244-1930, 5pm-midnight, Tues.-Sat.) is a long-term expat hangout with local microbrews and good Italian food.

Live folk music happens at **Ñucanchi Peña** (Universitario 496 at Armero, tel. 2/225-4096, 9pm-midnight Wed.-Thurs., 9pm-2am Fri.-Sat.), near the Santa Clara market.

Finn McCool's is a local favorite.

Alternatively, Quito's Old Town also has a few good spots to go out. The best are along the regenerated La Ronda, which is lined with restaurants, cafés, and bars, several of which offer live music on the weekend. One of these is Café Sibari (La Ronda 707, tel. 2/228-9809, 11am-midnight Mon.-Sat.), which has performances every night. Bandido Brewing (Olmedo E1-136 Pedro Fermín Cevallos, http://bandidobrewing.com, 2pm-midnight Wed.-Sat.) is Old Town's newest tap room, with a rotating variety of craft beer served in a converted chapel by its three friendly, expat owners. Weekly events such as Saturday barbecues make it a locals' secret worth discovering.

Wherever you go out, you cannot help but notice that Ecuadorians' dancing skills leave the rest of us looking like we have two left feet. You can do something about this—take the plunge and get some classes at one of these dancing schools: Academia Salsa and Merengue (Foch E4-256, tel. 2/222-0427), Ritmo Tropical Dance Academy (Amazonas N24-155 at Calama, tel. 2/255-7094, ritmotropical5@hotmail.com), Tropical Dancing School (Foch E4-256 at Amazonas, tel. 2/222-0427), and Son Latino (Reina Victoria N24-211 at Lizardo García, tel. 2/223-4340). Prices at all of these schools start at about $10 pp per hour for one-on-one or couples lessons.

THEATERS AND CONCERTS

The *El Comercio* newspaper runs information on theater performances and music concerts.

When possible, buying advance tickets is a good idea. The Casa de la Cultura (6 de Diciembre N16-224 at La Patria, tel. 2/290-2272, www.cce.org.ec) is the city's leading venue for theater, dance, and classical music. The colorful, indigenous-themed Jacchigua Ecuadorian Folklore Ballet (tel. 2/295-2025, www.jacchiguasecuador.com) performs here at 7:30pm Wednesday. Another good option for ballet and contemporary dance is Ballet Andino Humanizarte at Teatro Humanizarte (Leonidas Plaza N24-226 at Lizardo García, tel. 2/257-3486).

Quito has several excellent theaters. The 19th century Teatro Sucre (Plaza del Teatro, tel. 2/257-0299, www.teatrosucre. com) is Ecuador's national theater and one of the best. The Teatro Bolívar (Espejo 847 at Guayaquil, tel. 2/258-2486, www.teatrobolivar.org) is still under restoration following a devastating fire but should return to its former glory in the near future following substantial government investment.

The Teatro Politecnico (Ladrón de Guevara and Queseras) is the best place for classical music, hosting the National Symphony. The Patio de Comedias (18 de Septiembre 457 at Amazonas, tel. 2/256-1902) is a good spot to catch a play Thursday-Sunday in a more intimate atmosphere.

Quito's biggest rock and pop concerts take place at the Coliseo Rumiñahui and Estadio Olímpico. Many big-name acts from North and South America play at these prestigious venues. A good website for tickets to upcoming events is Ecutickets (www.ecutickets.ec).

Shopping

CRAFTS AND GALLERIES

New Town has the richest pickings for shoppers—almost every block in the Mariscal district has some sort of crafts shop or sidewalk vendor. Take your time, shop around, and compare quality. There are also a few standouts in Old Town.

Hungarian-born Olga Fisch came to Ecuador to escape the war in Europe in 1939. She became a world-renowned expert on South American crafts and folklore; during her lifetime, she was sought by the Smithsonian Institution and collectors worldwide for her advice. Folklore Olga Fisch (Colón E10-53 at Caamaño, tel./fax 2/254-1315, www.olgafisch.com, 9am-7pm Mon.-Fri., 10am-6pm Sat.) was her house until her death in 1991. The first floor is filled with gorgeous but pricey ceramics and textiles from all over the continent. Out back in what was once a storeroom is a restaurant called El Galpon. There are outlets of Fisch's shop in the Hilton Colón, the Swissôtel, and the Patio Andaluz in Old Town.

La Bodega (Juan León Mera and Carrión, tel. 2/222-5844) has been in business for over 30 years and stocks high-quality artisanal works that include adorable ceramic Galápagos creatures and jewelry. For suede and leather, try Aramis (Amazonas N24-32 at Pinto, tel. 2/222-8546), where they can make clothes or handbags to order.

Mindalae (Reina Victoria 17-80 at La Niña, tel. 2/223-0609) is also operated by the nonprofit Sinchi Sacha Foundation. It houses a shop selling indigenous crafts and a small restaurant. The Camari Cooperative (Marchena and 10 de Agosto, tel. 2/252-3613, www.camari.org) provides a place for indigenous and fair-trade groups from throughout Ecuador to sell their crafts. The store features a wide selection with good prices and quality.

Excedra (Carrión 243 at Tamayo, tel. 2/222-4001) serves as an art gallery, folklore and antique outlet, and tea room. It's an offbeat little place with a nice selection of crafts. Beautiful, high-quality wool textiles for less money than you'd think are the specialty at Hilana (6 de Diciembre 1921 at Baquerizo Moreno, tel. 2/254-0714).

The most popular place to buy paintings is Parque El Ejido Art Fair (Patria and Amazonas), open all day Saturday-Sunday. Most paintings for sale are imitations of more famous works, but there's a good range and excellent value. Haggling, of course, is advised.

Professional browsers could spend hours on Juan León Mera and Veintimilla, where half a dozen highbrow crafts and antiques stores and art galleries cluster within two blocks of Libri Mundi. Try Galería Latina (Juan León Mera N23-69, tel. 2/222-1098, www.galerialatina-quito.com) for Tigua hide paintings and other quality works, or stop by the weekend arts-and-crafts market in the park by Avenida Patria. Galería Beltrán (Reina Victoria 326, tel. 2/222-1732) has a good selection of paintings by Ecuadorian artists.

In Old Town, one of the best options is Tianguez (underneath the Iglesia San Francisco, Plaza San Francisco, tel. 2/223-0609, www.tianguez.org, 9am-6pm daily), which is run by the Sinchi Sacha Foundation, a nonprofit set up to help support the people of the Oriente. The store, which also has an outdoor café on the Plaza San Francisco, features an excellent selection of quality handicrafts from around the country for surprisingly low prices. Profits from the masks, ceramics, Tigua hide paintings, jewelry, and weavings go to fund their programs to benefit indigenous communities.

Hugo Chiliquinga (Huachi N67-34 at Legarda, tel. 2/259-8822) is considered by many to be the best guitar maker in Ecuador. He makes and sells guitars, but he may have a waiting list, since he has an international reputation.

BOOKS

Libri Mundi (Juan León Mera N23-83 at Wilson, tel. 2/223-4791, www.librimundi. com, 8:30am-7pm Mon.-Fri., 10am-4pm Sat.) is probably the best bookstore in Ecuador. Along with a wide range of titles in Spanish, it sells new and a few used English, German, and French foreign books at a markup. Libri Mundi also has branches in the Plaza del Quindé, Centro Comercial Quicentro, and in Cumbayá.

For great deals on secondhand books, have a free cup of tea at the friendly English-run English Bookshop (Calama and Almagro, 10am-6:30pm daily). Mark, the owner, is also a great source of information for anything related to Ecuador. Confederate Books (Calama 410 at Juan León Mera, tel. 2/252-7890, 10am-6pm Mon.-Sat.) also has a wide range of used books.

MAGAZINES AND NEWSPAPERS

Foreign magazines fill the shelves at Libro Express (Amazonas 816 at Veintimilla, tel. 2/254-8113, 9:30am-7:30pm Mon.-Fri., 10am-6pm Mon.-Sat.). Street vendors all along Amazonas also stock a few foreign publications. Bookshops in expensive hotels sell foreign magazines and newspapers, but be sure they don't try to mark up the newspapers over the printed price.

SPORTING EQUIPMENT

If you're looking for a mask and snorkel (or even a wetsuit) for your Galápagos trip, you'll find them—along with a whole store full of modern sporting equipment—at KAO Sport (Ed. Ecuatoriana, Almagro and Colón, tel. 2/255-0005 or 2/252-2266). Other KAO branches are located in many of the city's *centros comerciales*.

JEWELRY AND ACCESSORIES

Marcel G. Creaciones (Roca 766, between Amazonas and 9 de Octubre, tel. 2/265-3555, fax 2/255-2672) carries a good selection of Panama hats. For exclusive jewelry designs, stop by the Museo Fundación Guayasamín (Bosmediano 543, tel. 2/244-6455, 10am-5pm Mon.-Fri.) or Ag (Juan León Mera 614 at Carrión, tel. 2/255-0276, fax 2/250-2301). Many small leather-working shops in New Town can make custom clothes, boots, bags, and other accessories for surprisingly reasonable prices; try Zapytal (Pinto 538 at Amazonas, tel. 2/252-8757).

MARKETS

Vendors have been moved off the streets, making driving and walking around the city much easier, if a little less colorful. For street-side shopping in Old Town, go to Ipiales (clothing and shoes), Calle Cuenca between Mejía and Olmedo (crafts and bazaar items), San Roque (food and furniture), and Plaza Arenas ("recycled" stolen goods, clothes, and hardware). There are a lot of pickpockets, so watch your wallet, and ideally don't take valuables and cameras when you go to a market.

On weekends, the north end of Parque El Ejido becomes an outdoor art gallery with a selection of paintings, sculpture, and jewelry. La Mariscal artisan market in New Town occupies half of the block south of Jorge Washington between Reina Victoria and Juan León Mera. Just about every indigenous craft in Ecuador makes an appearance daily. Quality is variable, and haggling is obligatory.

On Saturdays, local artists gather in Plaza Foch to sell paintings, carvings, jewelry, and handicrafts.

Local produce is the main draw to New Town's Mercado Santa Clara (biggest market on Wed. and Sun.), along Ulloa and Versalles just south of Colón. Every Friday, a fruit and vegetable market fills Galaviz between Toledo and Isabel La Católica, where children sell baskets of spices and wealthy shoppers hire elderly basket carriers to tote the day's purchases.

Boutiques, supermarkets, and movie theaters find a home in Quito's many *centros comerciales* (malls). Close your eyes and you could be in North America. Major malls include El Bosque (Al Parque and Alonso de Torres), El Jardín (República and Amazonas), Iñaquito (Amazonas and Naciones Unidas), Multicentro (6 de Diciembre and La Niña), CC Nu (Naciones Unidas and Amazonas), and Quicentro (6 de Diciembre and Naciones Unidas); and in the south, the El Recreo trolley terminus and Quitumbe bus terminal.

Sports and Recreation

CLIMBING AND MOUNTAINEERING
Climbing Companies
A few of the many tour companies in Quito specialize in climbing—they have the experience and professionalism to get you back down in one piece should anything go wrong. Prices for these climbing tours vary from $70 per person for easier climbs, such as the Pichinchas, to $220-350 per person for a two-day ascent of Cotopaxi.

Andean Face (Avenida Universitaria Km. 3 1/2 S/N, Conjunto Vista de Los Andes, Casa #1, La Tola Chica, Tumbaco, tel. 2/205-2194, www.andeanface.com) is a Dutch-Ecuadorian company specializing in climbing whose guides are often on loan to Everest summits. They can arrange anything from a Cotopaxi trek to a several-week-long trip to all of the peaks in the country. The Compañía de Guías (Jorge Washington 425 at 6 de Diciembre, tel. 2/255-6210, tel./fax 2/250-4773, guisamontania@accessinter.net, www.companiadeguias.com) is a guide cooperative whose members speak English, German, French, and Italian. Ecuadorian Alpine Institute (Ramírez Dávalos 136 at Amazonas, Of. 102, tel. 2/256-5465, www.volcanoclimbing.com) has well-organized, professionally run climbs and treks, and spans all experience levels. Safari Tours (Edificio Banco de Guayaquil, 11th Fl., Reina Victoria y Colón, tel. 2/255-2505, fax 2/222-3381, tel./fax 2/222-0426, www.safari.com.ec) has highly recommended climbing trips to any peak in the country, plus a range of other tours.

Sierra Nevada (Pinto 637 at Cordero, tel. 2/255-3658 or 2/222-4717, fax 2/255-4936, www.hotelsierranevada.com) is a small, dependable operator that also offers rafting, the Galápagos, and Amazon trips.

Climbing and Camping Equipment
Quito has by far the best selection of outdoor gear merchants in the country. Everything from plastic climbing boots and harnesses to tents, sleeping bags, and stoves is readily available, although not always of the highest quality or best state of repair. Needless to say, check all zippers, laces, and fuel valves before you head off into the wild. Large-size footgear (U.S. size 12 and up) may be hard to locate. Gear is both imported (at a high markup) or made in Ecuador.

For climbing gear for sale or rent, try Altamontaña (Jorge Washington 425 at 6 de Diciembre, tel. 2/255-8380) or Antisana Sport (tel./fax 2/246-7433) in the El Bosque Shopping Center, also good for large-size hiking boots. Other places to buy camping gear include Camping Cotopaxi (Colón 942 at Reina Victoria, tel. 2/252-1626), The Explorer (Reina Victoria 928 at Pinto, tel. 2/255-0911), and Los Alpes (Reina Victoria 2345 at Baquedano, tel./fax 2/223-2326). Equipos Cotopaxi (6 de Diciembre N20-36 at Jorge Washington, tel. 2/225-0038) makes its own sleeping bags, backpacks, and tents for less than you'd pay for imported items. The various Marathon Sports outlets in the Centros Comerciales El Bosque, El Jardín,

Iñaquito, San Rafael, and Quicentro stock light-use sportswear at decent prices.

BIKING

The Aries Bike Company (Av. Interoceanica Km. 22.5, Vía Pifo, La Libertad, tel. 2/238-0802, www.ariesbikecompany.com) offers 1-14-day biking and hiking tours all over Ecuador. The guides speak English, Dutch, and Spanish.

Biking Dutchman (Foch 714 at Juan León Mera, tel. 2/254-2806, www.biking-dutchman.com) runs well-reviewed day trips to Cotopaxi, Papallacta, and the Tandayapa-Mindo area. The 30-kilometer descent down Cotopaxi is guaranteed to raise your blood pressure. There are two-day trips to Cotopaxi and Quilotoa as well as the upper Amazon, and tours of up to eight days are offered.

Every Sunday, a long north-south section of road through Quito is closed to cars and open only to cyclists, skateboarders, skaters, and walkers. Biciacción (Psje. Rumipamba S/N y Av. De Los Shyris, tel. 2/332-4004) rents bicycles from one hour ($2) to a full day ($15) and also offers a few different city tours ($30).

RAFTING AND KAYAKING

Yacu Amu Rafting (Foch 746 at Juan León Mera, tel. 2/290-4054, fax 2/290-4055, www.yacuamu.com) is the leader in white-water trips out of Quito. The year-round day trips down the Toachi and Blanco Rivers offer more rapids per hour than anywhere else in Ecuador ($79 pp Toachi, $89 pp Quijos)—plus cold beer at the end of every trip. Two-day trips cost from $219 pp, and five-day trips on the Upano are offered August-February. Customized itineraries are possible, as are kayak rentals and kayak courses.

HORSEBACK RIDING

Sally Vergette runs Ride Andes (tel. 9/973-8221, www.rideandes.com), offering top-quality riding tours through the highlands. From the foothills of Imbabura to cattle round-ups near Cotopaxi, the trips use local horse wranglers, support vehicles, and healthy, happy animals. Guests stay in some of the country's plushest haciendas along the way. The options range from $110 pp for two people on a one-day tour to an eight-day circuit of Cotopaxi for $1,998 pp. You must have some riding experience for the longer tours, but it's worth it to experience the scenery from atop a horse.

Astrid Müller of the Green Horse Ranch (tel. 8/612-5433, www.horseranch.de) offers riding trips starting in Pululahua Crater from $85 pp for one day, $230 pp for two days, and up to $1,620 pp for an eight-day tour in the highlands and cloud forests. These are for people of all experience levels, and the prices include food, accommodations, and transportation to and from Quito. Multilingual guides accompany all trips.

SPECTATOR SPORTS

Watching a soccer match (called *fútbol* or football outside the United States) in Ecuador is quite an experience. Witnessing the fervor of the fans firsthand can be exhilarating. The best place to go in Quito is the Estadio Atahualpa (6 de Diciembre and Naciones Unidas) when the national team plays. Take the Ecovia to the Naciones Unidas stop to get there. The Casa Blanca, which is the stadium of Liga de Quito, the city's most successful club, has home games several times per month. Buy tickets ahead of time at Casa Blanca at the "Y" junction, and take the Metrovía bus to the Ofelia terminal.

CITY TOURS

The Quito Tour Bus (tel. 2/435-458, www.quitotourbus.com, 9am-4pm daily, $12) offers a hop on-hop off bus service with 12 stops across the city including Plaza Grande, La Compañía, El Panecillo, La Basilica, the telefériqo and a few of the major parks in the city. Audio is available in in English, Spanish, French and German. Tickets can be bought at a few points across the city, the easiest being outside República del Cacao on Plaza Foch in the Mariscal. Night tours are offered

Tour Companies

Quito has more tour companies than ever, and many of them are excellent. For a price, they offer expertise and local knowledge that you can't find elsewhere and provide a rewarding experience that would be difficult to replicate independently. Taking a guided tour also takes the worry out of traveling: Accommodations, food, and logistics are all sorted out for you. Bear in mind that not all operators in Quito have good reputations: Some overcharge and are underqualified. The following are recommended for their quality, professionalism, and value. (Please note that it is not uncommon for companies to ask for payment by wire transfer or PayPal due to the unreliable service of credit card companies in Ecuador.)

- **Enchanted Expeditions** (de las Alondras N45-102 at Los Lirios, tel. 2/334-0525, fax 2/334-0123, www.enchantedexpeditions.com) covers the entire country, with a focus on the Galápagos—the boats *Cachalote* and *Beluga* receive frequent praise.

- **Galapagos Travel Center** is currently the best run tour operator in the country for Galápagos tours. The company has branched out to include just about every kind of tour in Ecuador, including hacienda stays, community visits, city and market tours, and train trips. Its main office is in Quito (Plaza Foch, next to Nü House Hotel, tel. 2/290-9394, http://ecuador.galapagosislands.com).

- **Gulliver Expeditions** (Juan Leon Mera N24-156 y José Calama, tel. 2/252-8030, www.gulliver.com.ec) offers deluxe package tours including mountain biking, 4x4 off-road, and luxury treks across Ecuador.

- **Happy Gringo Travel** (Oficina 207, Edificio Catalina Plaza, Aldaz N34-155 & Portugal, tel. 2/512-3486, www.happygringo.com) is best known for its Cuyabeno trips of three, four, and five days.

- **Nuevo Mundo Travel and Tours** (18 de Septiembre E4-161 at Juan León Mera, tel. 2/255-3826, www.nuevomundotravel.com) was started in 1979 by a founder and former president of the Ecuadorian Ecotourism Association. Its tours and facilities are therefore among the most environmentally conscious in Ecuador—the company doesn't even advertise some of them to minimize impact on the destinations. Along with the usual Galápagos and Oriente tours, several unique options include shamanism programs and one-month Spanish courses combined with environmental studies.

- **RainForestur** (Amazonas N4-20 at Robles, tel./fax 2/223-9822, www.rainforestur.com) has received praise for its Cuyabeno trips and rafting in Baños, but there's also a full slate of other options.

- **Safari Tours** (Av. Del Establo 181 and Las Garzas Cumbaya, tel. 2/255-2505, U.S./Canada tel. 866/247-2405, www.safari.com.ec) is one of the most frequently recommended operators in the country and can take you just about anywhere in Ecuador to climb, hike, bird-watch, camp, or mountain bike. Safari has a complete Galápagos database and can book last-minute spaces or make reservations online.

- **Sangay Touring** (Amazonas 1188 and Cordero, tel. 2/222-1336, tel./fax. 2/226-0406, www.sangay.com) is a British- and Ecuadorian-run agency that has been offering tours around the country since 1992. Sangay recently split off a sister company, Guide2Galapagos (www.guide2galapagos.com) to handle island bookings.

- **Surtrek** (Reina Victoria N24-151 and Calama, tel. 800/787-873, www.surtrek.org) offers a wide range of Galápagos and Amazon tours, as well as trekking, climbing, cycling, and rafting.

- **Tropic Journeys in Nature** (Pasaje Sanches Melo OE1-37 y Av. Galo Plaza Lasso, tel. 2/240-8741, in the U.S. tel. 202/657-5072, www.destinationecuador.com) is run by Andy Drumm, a fellow of the Royal Geographic Society and the president of the Amazon Commission of the Ecuadorian Ecotourism Association. These trips have won awards for socially responsible tourism and are especially strong in the Oriente, where they introduce travelers to the Huaorani, Cofán, and Achuar.

on Fridays, Saturdays and holidays from 7pm-10pm.

Ecuador Freedom Bike Rentals (Juan León Mera N22-37, tel. 2/250-4339, www. freedombikerental.com, 10am-6pm daily, $35 plus deposit) offer self-guided GPS scooter tours of the city and surrounding areas. Tours are customized to the rider and all equipment is provided.

For an off-the-beaten path view of Quito, Happy Gringo's **Half Day Reality Tour** (Oficina 207, Edificio Catalina Plaza, Catalina Aldaz N34-155 and Portugal, tel. 2/512-2346, eva@happygringo.com, 9am-6pm Mon.-Fri., $30-45) takes you to markets, confectionary makers, historic La Ronda, and art galleries for a view into the seldom-seen side of Quito.

Carpe Diem Adventures offers a free **Old Town Walking Tour** (Antepara E4-70 y Los Rios, tel. 2/295-4713,www.carpedm. ca,10:30am Mon.-Fri.) that explores the plazas, churches, and sights built by the Spanish during their tenure in Quito. Tours leave from the Secret Garden hostel.

Accommodations

As Ecuador's capital and tourism hub, Quito has an enormous range of accommodations, from bargain basement to lavish luxury. Most are found in New Town, although Old Town has more historic hotels.

Reservations are a good idea at busy times, such as holidays, especially Christmas and Easter. Book by phone or email whenever possible. A tax of up to 22 percent will be added to bills in the more expensive hotels, and a separate charge may be tacked on for paying by credit card. Also bear in mind that some hostels don't include the required 12 percent tax on their listed prices. Check ahead of time to avoid an unwanted surprise.

UNDER $10

The constant stream of backpackers through Quito means that competition is fierce and there is a huge range of budget accommodations. Most are very good value and are concentrated in New Town.

New Town

French Canadian-owned **El Centro del Mundo** (Lizardo García 569 at Reina Victoria, tel. 2/222-9050, www.centrodelmundo.net, $6 dorm, $8 s, $15 d) is one of the most popular backpacker crash pads and has rock-bottom prices. The small rooftop patio features cooking facilities, and the cable TV is always on in the cushion-strewn common room. It gets pretty raucous on the free rum-and-coke nights. Breakfast and Internet access are included. **The Backpacker's Inn** (Juan Rodriguez E7-48 at Reina Victoria, tel. 2/250-9669, www.backpackersinn.net, $7.50 dorm, $11 s, $22 d) is a quieter budget option with simple, decent guest rooms, a laundry area, free Internet, and TV in the lounge. **Hostal New Bask** (Lizardo García and Diego de Almagro, tel. 2/256-7153, www. newhostalbask.com, $8 dorm, $18 s or d) is another quiet option with a homey atmosphere, excellent-value guest rooms, and a small lounge.

Hostal Blue House (Pinto and Diego de Almagro, tel. 2/222-3480, www.bluehousequito.com, $8-9 dorm, $18 s, $24-30 d) is a very popular backpacker hostel with a kitchen, a bar, free Internet, and breakfast included. A cozy option is **El Cafécito** (Cordero 1124 at Reina Victoria, tel. 2/223-4862, www.cafecito.net, $7 dorm, $10-15 s, $25 d), which has guest rooms above a popular café. The small and inviting **Hostal Posada del Maple** (Juan Rodriguez E8-49 at 6 de Diciembre, tel. 2/290-7367, www.posadadelmaple.com, $9 dorm, $21 s, $26-36 d, breakfast included) is an attractive place with balconies and a plant-filled courtyard. Breakfast is big, and there's a comfortable TV room.

Old Town

Most of Old Town's options are in the mid- and expensive range, but **Hostal Sucre** (Bolívar 615 at Cuenca, tel. 2/295-4025, $4-10 pp) bucks the trend. It's astonishing that such a cheap place is right on Plaza San Francisco with views of the square. For these prices and location, you can't expect more than cheap, shabby guest rooms, but the view and the friendly atmosphere make it a worthwhile choice.

$10-25

All hotels below offer guest rooms with private baths unless otherwise noted.

New Town

Hostal El Vagabundo (Wilson E7-45, tel. 2/222-6376, $13 s, $22 d) is another dependable budget option with a small café and table tennis. The **Loro Verde** (Rodriguez 241 at Almagro, tel. 2/222-6173, www.hostaloroverde.com, $16 s, $30 d, breakfast included) is as colorful and chirpy as its name ("green parrot"). On a corner of Mariscal's main artery, the **Amazonas Inn** (Pinto 471 at Amazonas, tel. 2/2908699, $16 s, $28 d) is a friendly hotel with comfortable if compact guest rooms with cable TV.

You don't have to stay in Mariscal; a few blocks uphill from New Town is a neighborhood called La Floresta. Not to be confused with La Casona in Old Town, **La Casona de Mario** (Andalucia 213 at Galicia, tel./fax 2/223-0129 or 2/254-4036, www.casonademario.com, $12 pp) is run by a friendly Argentine in a comfortable house with a garden, a kitchen, a patio, and laundry facilities. Also in La Floresta is **Aleida's Hostal** (Andalucia 559, tel. 2/223-4570, www.aleidashostal.com.ec, $17-25 s, $30-36 d), a friendly family-run guesthouse with large guest rooms.

Old Town

Hidden away on a quiet street northeast of Old Town is Aussie-owned backpacker favorite **Secret Garden** (Antepara E4-60 at Los Rios, tel. 2/295-6704, www.secretgardenquito.com,

$11-13 dorm, $30 s and d). Set on five floors in a UNESCO World Heritage-listed building, TV is shunned for music and murals. The rooftop terrace has an impressive view, and there are big breakfasts and organic food for reasonable prices. It's a great place to meet other travelers in a relaxed setting.

Overlooking Old Town, **Minka Hostal** (Matovelle 219 between Venezuela y Vargas, tel. 9/9662-6889, www.minkahostel.com, $10-12 pp, breakfast included) offers comfortable dorms for backpackers. Services include kitchen facilities, luggage storage, and weekly events.

Casa Bambu (Solano E527 and Ave. Gran Colombia, tel. 2/222-8738, http://hotelbambuecuador.com, $10 dorm, $25 s, $35 d) has two staggered terraces overlooking Parque El Ejido, a guest kitchen, and Internet. Its location is between Old and New Town and is on a steep hill, so take a taxi if carrying big bags.

The **Hostal San Blas** (Caldas E1-38 and Pedro Fermin Cevallos, tel. 2/228-9480, $15 s, $27 d) offers good service with guest rooms around an interior patio. Just before the southbound Plaza del Teatro *trole* stop, the **Hotel Plaza del Teatro** (Guayaquil 1373 at Esmeraldas, tel. 2/295-9462 or 2/295-4293, $14 pp) is a great value. The plush reception area leads to charming if slightly worn guest rooms.

$25-50

All hotels in this category and up include breakfast in the price unless otherwise indicated.

New Town

A small rise in price brings you into the realm of charming old guesthouses with all the amenities and a healthy dose of character. **Hotel Plaza Internacional** (Leonidas Plaza 150 at 18 de Septiembre, tel. 2/252-4530, tel./fax 2/250-5075, www.hotelplazainternacional.com, $30 s, $40 d) is the attractive colonial home of two former presidents. Staff speak English, French, and Portuguese. **Hostal El Arupo** (Juan Rodriguez E7-22 at Reina

Victoria, tel. 2/255-7543, $30 s, $45 d) is an attractive renovated house with colorful rooms, and nearby Cayman Hotel (Juan Rodriguez 270 at Reina Victoria, tel. 2/256-7616, www. hotelcaymanquito.com, $35 s, $55 d) has a similar offering with a huge fireplace, a large garden, and a good restaurant inside a renovated house. Jardín del Sol (Calama E8-29 at Almagro, tel. 2/223-0941, www.hostaljardindelsol.com, $40 s, $50 d) has decent guest rooms, some with balconies. The rear guest rooms are quieter.

Wooden floors and a cozy atmosphere await visitors to the Casa Sol (Calama 127 at 6 de Diciembre, tel. 2/223-0798, www.lacasasol.com, $48 s, $68 d), a cheery spot with a tiny courtyard owned by *indígenas* from Peguche, near Otavalo. They have a TV room and a book exchange in front of a fireplace.

Old Town

A former colonial home, the ★ Hotel San Francisco de Quito (Sucre 217 at Guayaquil, tel. 2/228-7758, tel./fax 2/295-1241, www.sanfranciscodequito.com.ec, $30 s, $50 d) is the pick of Old Town's mid-range options, with a fountain and ferns filling the courtyard and a rooftop patio with great views. Tucked upstairs facing La Concepción Church is the renovated Posada Colonial (García Moreno and Chile, tel. 2/228-1095, $26 s, $36 d), with comfortable guest rooms that have classic decor and tall ceilings. Hotel Catedral (Mejia 638 at Benalcázar, tel. 2/295-5438, www.hotelcatedral.ec, $31 s, $55 d) offers comfortable guest rooms, cable TV, a sauna, and a steam room. Hotel Real Audiencia (Bolívar 220 at Guayaquil, tel. 2/295-2711 or 2/295-0590, www.realaudiencia.com, $33 s, $52 d) has stylish guest rooms, black-and-white photography on the walls, and a great view of Plaza Santo Domingo.

$50-75
New Town

Thick fur rugs in front of the fireplace add to the Old World feel of Hostal Los Alpes (Tamayo 233 at Jorge Washington, tel./fax

2/256-1110, www.hotellosalpes.com, $67 s, $80 d). The bright and clean Hostal de La Rábida (La Rábida 227 at Santa María, tel./fax 2/222-2169, www.hostalrabida.com, $71 s, $91 d) has an immaculate white interior and stylish carpeted rooms. There's a fireplace in the living room and a peaceful garden out back.

★ Fuente de Piedra II (Juan León Mera and Baquedano, tel. 2/290-0323, $56-67) is a place to treat yourself. This colonial-style mid-range hotel is elegantly furnished with attentive service, Wi-Fi, and a gourmet restaurant. A sister hotel is at Tamayo and Wilson.

$75-100
New Town

A nine-story building is home to the Hotel Sebastián (Almagro 822 at Cordero, tel. 2/222-2300, fax 2/222-2500, www.hotelsebastian.com, $90 s, $100 d, not including breakfast), which uses organic vegetables in its restaurant; the building boasts one of the best water-purification systems in the country.

★ Café Cultura (Robles 513 at Reina Victoria, tel./fax 2/256-4956, www.cafecultura.com, $100 s, $122 d) is set in a beautifully restored colonial mansion, formerly the French cultural center. The hotel is lovingly decorated with dark wood, paintings, and a grand staircase in the center of it all. Guest rooms are uniquely decorated, and the bathrooms are huge, with tubs for relaxing after a hard day's sightseeing. There's a gourmet café downstairs, a small private garden out back, a library full of guidebooks, and three stone fireplaces for those cold Quito nights. Breakfast is not included in the room price.

Old Town

Hotel Casa Gardenia (Calle Benalcazar N9-42 and Oriente, tel. 2/295-7936, www.hotelcasagardenia.com, $89 s, $122 d) is a stylish addition to Old Town set in a restored colonial house. Nine modern rooms with balconies overlooking the Basílica surround an inside courtyard. The top-notch amenities, the view of Old Town, and the friendly staff make staying here a pleasure.

$100-200
New Town

The huge Hotel Quito (González Suárez N27-142 at 12 de Octubre, tel. 2/396-4900, fax 2/256-7284, www.hotelquito.com, $111 s, $148 d, not including breakfast) boasts one of the best views in Quito, high on a hill above Guapulo. The guest rooms have recently been refurbished and there is plenty to keep you busy—a swimming pool, a spa, and a gourmet restaurant.

The 415 guest rooms and suites of the Hilton Colón (Amazonas 110 at Patria, tel. 2/256-0666, fax 2/256-3903, U.S. tel. 800/HILTONS—800/445-8667, www.hiltoncolon.com, $209 s or d, not including breakfast) tower over the Parque El Ejido, and it's probably the most popular spot for visitors who have unlimited budgets. Facilities include an excellent gym, a 10-meter pool, a reading room, and shops.

Mariscal now has its very own slice of boutique chic in the shape of the Nu House (Foch E6-12, tel. 2/255-7485, www.nuhousehotels.com, $145 s, $189 d). This wood-and-glass building rises high over the main plaza. Guest rooms have huge windows and dramatic color schemes, and there's a spa.

Perhaps the largest luxury hotel in Quito is the JW Marriott Hotel Quito (Orellana 1172 at Amazonas, tel. 2/297-2000, fax 2/297-2050, www.marriott.com, $162 s or d). This glass palace contains 257 guest rooms and 16 suites, a business center, an outdoor heated pool, a health club, and a Mediterranean restaurant.

Old Town

Once a family home, El Relicario del Carmen (Venezuela and Olmedo, tel. 2/228-9120, www.hotelrelicariodelcarmen.com, $105 s, $135 d) has been meticulously renovated and made into a comfortable retreat for travelers who want to stay in the colonial part of the city. The abundant artwork and stained glass windows are particular highlights.

Patio Andaluz (García Moreno and Olmedo, tel. 2/228-0830, www.hotelpatio-andaluz.com, $200 s or d) is the fruit of a massive project that restored a 16th-century colonial home with two interior patios, spacious guest rooms, and split-level suites. An excellent restaurant is on the first-floor patio with carved stone pillars. Service is understandably top-notch.

OVER $200
New Town

Uphill from the Hilton Colón to the east, the Swissôtel (12 de Octubre 1820 at Cordero, tel. 2/256-7600, fax 2/256-8079, http://quito.swissotel.com, $250 s, $265 d) has 277 wheelchair-accessible guest rooms and a private health club, along with Japanese and Italian restaurants and a gourmet deli.

Old Town

Quito's first hotel and still one of its best is Plaza Grande (García Moreno and Chile, tel. 2/251-0777, U.S. tel. 888/790-5264, www.plazagrandequito.com, $500 s or d) on the main square. It has 15 suites, three restaurants, a ballroom, champagne and brandy bars, chandeliers, and luxurious guest rooms with the marble bathroom floors and jetted tubs.

Outside Town

Located 15 minutes out of town and nestled in the hills on the Volcán Pichincha side of the valley, the luxurious Hacienda Rumiloma (tel. 2/320-0953, www.rumiloma.com, $355-725) offers Old World charm with lavishly appointed rooms and suites, a fine dining restaurant with Andean and coastal specialties, and over 200 bottles handpicked from across the continent. Elsewhere in the hacienda is a genuine Irish pub. Hacienda Rumiloma is located east of town, at the very end of Calle Obispo Diaz de la Madrid.

LONGER STAYS

Most hotels will arrange a discount for stays of a few weeks or more. For example, the Residencial Casa Oriente (Yaguachi 824 at Llona, tel. 2/254-6157) offers apartments with or without kitchens for $115-200 per month with a minimum stay of two weeks. Spanish lessons are available, and English, French, and German are spoken. **St. Gallen Haus** (Guanguiltagua N37-04 at Diego Noboa, www.stgallenhaus.com) is located in the scenic El Batan neighborhood, north of New Town and away from the fray. The modern complex has single and double rooms with shared or private baths and shared suites and apartments ranging from $120 per week to $450 per month. **La Posada de Guapulo** (Leonidas Plaza E16-160 y Calvario, tel. 098/460-6267), in the friendly neighborhood of Guapulo, is another housing option for those looking for peace and quiet. Rooms are well-appointed with private bathrooms for $200 a month.

For a more authentic cultural experience, a **family stay** is a great way to practice your Spanish and get to know Ecuadorian culture from the inside. It is often just as affordable as a budget hotel as long as you are willing to make a longer commitment. Check with Spanish schools for their recommendations as they normally have a list of families they trust with their students.

Food

Quito has the widest range of international restaurants in Ecuador as well as many excellent local eateries. Here you will find the biggest diversity of world cuisine: from Asian curries to Italian pasta, Mexican fajitas to Argentine steaks, and there are plenty of cheap cafés, fast food joints, and $3 set-menus for those on a tighter budget. Many restaurants outside New Town close by 9 or 10pm and throughout the city many are closed on Sundays. Note also that it's surprisingly difficult to find an early breakfast in New Town as most places open at 8am.

OLD TOWN
Bakeries, Cafés, and Snacks
There are plenty of cozy little bakeries to pop into between sights in Old Town. At the entrance of San Agustin Monastery is **El Cafeto** (Chile and Guayaquil, no phone, 8am-7:30pm Mon.-Sat., 8am-noon Sun.), specializing in coffee and hot chocolate served with *humitas,* tamales, empanadas, and cakes. In the courtyard of the Centro Cultural Metropolitano, **El Búho** (José Moreno and Espejo, tel. 2/228-9877, 11am-7pm Mon.-Thurs., 11am-9pm Fri.-Sat., noon-5pm Sun., $3-6) is a quiet spot for a snack with a range of soups, salads, sandwiches, and pasta.

Old Town has several great ice cream parlors. **Frutería Monserrate** (Espejo Oe2-12, tel. 2/258-3408, 8am-7:30pm Mon.-Fri., 9am-6:30pm Sat.-Sun., $2-5) serves extravagant helpings of fruit salad and ice cream as well as cheap lunches and sandwiches. **Heladería San Agustin** (Guayaquil 1053, tel. 2/228-5082, 9am-6pm Mon.-Fri., 9am-4pm Sat., 10am-3pm Sun., ice cream $1.50) claims to be the oldest in the city, having made *helados de paila* sorbets in copper bowls for 150 years.

Ecuadorian
Old Town has plenty of places for cheap set meals, but quality varies widely. On Plaza Grande, a small food court on Chile has a range of restaurants offering well-prepared local specialties. Just down the hill from Plaza Grande, **La Guaragua** (Espejo Oe2-40, tel. 2/257-2552, 10am-9pm Mon.-Thurs., 10am-11pm Fri.-Sun., entrées $3-6) is one of several restaurants offering local specialties from chicken stew to fried pork chops with beans. With live music Thursday-Saturday and 360-degree views over the colonial city, the **Vista Hermoso** (Mejía 453 at García Moreno, tel. 2/295-1401, Mon.-Sat. 3pm-midnight, entrées $6-10) offers pizzas, snacks, and cocktails on its rooftop terrace. Bring a jacket at night.

Supermarkets

Supermaxi is the city's biggest supermarket, with branches at La Niña and Yanes Pinzón, one block off 6 de Diciembre, as well as in the Centros Comerciales El Bosque, Iñaquito, Multicentro, América, El Jardín, and El Recreo, among others. The biggest **Megamaxi** branch is at 6 de Diciembre and Julio Moreno. **Mi Comisariato** is in the Centro Commercial Quicentro, at García Moreno and Mejía, and at Nuñez de Vela and Ignacio San María. They're all open 9am-7 or 8pm Monday-Saturday and close earlier on Sunday. The **Santa María** stores (8am-8pm daily) are a little cheaper; there are two in the north on Versalles and in Centro Commercial Iñaquito, as well as in the center at Venezuela and Sucre.

Organicatessen de Quito, located on the west side of Parque Carolina (Atahualpa E2-97 y Núñez de Vela, tel. 2/224-4854, 9am-6pm Mon.-Fri) is the retail outlet of the Andean Women and Family Foundation, Fundamyf, which works with over 10,000 producers of organic food in rural areas of Ecuador as a fair trade exporter.

On Plaza San Francisco, under the arches below the monastery is the ideally situated café **Tianguez** (Plaza San Francisco, tel. 2/295-4326, www.tianguez.org, 10am-6pm Mon.-Tues., 10am-11pm Wed.-Sun., entrées $3-5). After browsing the eclectic gift shop, choose from traditional snacks such as tamales and well-presented entrées such as *fritada* and *llapingachos*.

La Cuchara De San Marcos (Calle Junín E3-121, tel. 2/340-4667, noon-10pm Tues.-Sat., $4-12) is a local favorite tucked away down a dead-end street past Monastery Santa Catalina. They serve tasty vegetarian cuisine as well as carnivore-friendly dishes.

International

Part of colonial Quito's recent renaissance is an upsurge in high-end eateries. For a gourmet meal, look no further than the cozy cellar setting of ★ **Las Cuevas de Luis Candela** (Benalcázar 713 at Chile, tel. 2/228-7710, 10am-11pm daily, entrées $7-10), which has been attracting Quito's wealthy patrons since the 1960s. Paella and fondue bourguignonne are just two of the specialties. **Theatrum** (Manabi N8-131, tel. 2/257-1011 or 2/228-9669, www.theatrum.com.ec, 12:30pm-4:30pm and 7pm-11pm Mon.-Fri., 7pm-11pm Sat.-Sun., entrées $10-15), on the second floor of the Teatro Sucre, is another of the city's most elegant dining experiences, serving extravagantly presented gourmet dishes such as

barbecued octopus, crab ravioli, and rabbit risotto in a stylish setting. **Mea Culpa** (Chile and García Moreno, tel. 2/257-1011, 12:30pm-3:30pm and 7pm-11pm Mon.-Fri., 7pm-11pm Sat.-Sun., entrées $10-20), which overlooks the Plaza Grande, has a strict dress code, so leave your sneakers and jeans at home if you want to try out the special fare, such as ostrich with brandy and apple.

Beneath the Itchimbía Cultural Center is ★ **Mosaico** (Samaniego N8-95 at Antepara, tel. 2/254-2871, 11am-11pm daily, entrées $9-12), which is best for drinks at sunset, when the views of Old Town are unbeatable from the mosaic-inlaid tables on the terrace. Arrive early to secure a table, because this stylish spot fills up quickly with Quito's elite. A taxi from Old Town is $2.

Vegetarian food is harder to come by in Old Town than in Mariscal, but **Govindas** (Esmeraldas 853, tel. 2/296-6844, 8am-4pm Mon.-Sat., entrées $2-3) is 100 percent meat-free and has a wide range of lunches such as vegetable risotto and plenty of fresh yogurt and granola for breakfast.

Located in the corner of a 17th century convent, ★ **Café Dios No Muere** (Flores and Junin, Quito, tel. 2/257-1995, noon-10pm Mon.-Sat., entrées $9-12) is a small, vertical café offering Cajun specialties, cheese, and meat platters and sandwiches. The owner, Matt, is from Louisiana and is normally on hand to make sure that everything is just right.

NEW TOWN
Asian

Hundreds of inexpensive *chifas* fill the city, but most are barely adequate. Chifa Mayflower (Carrión 442 at 6 de Diciembre, tel. 2/254-0510, www.mayflower.com.ec, 11am-11pm daily, entrées $3-7) has received good reviews from celebrity chefs and is one of seven in this Quito chain, which includes branches in the El Bosque, El Jardín, Quicentro, and El Recreo malls. Portions of fried rice and noodles are large, and there are plenty of veggie dishes.

For sushi, expect to pay out. Noe Sushi Bar (Isabel la Católica N24-6274 y Coruña, tel. 2/322-8146, 12:30pm-3:30pm and 6:30pm-11:30pm daily, entrées $10-20) is one of the best in town, with excellent combination platters and sashimi. Sake (Rivet N30-166, tel. 2/252-4818, 12:30pm-3pm and 6:30pm-11pm daily, entrées $15-25) is also very good.

Mariscal offers several restaurants offering Asian specialties that you would struggle to find anywhere else in Ecuador. For curries, you can't beat ★ Chandani Tandoori (Juan León Mera and Cordero, tel. 2/222-1053, noon-10pm Mon.-Sat., noon-5pm Sun., entrées $3-5). Everything from *dopiaza* to korma, tikka masala, and *balti* is done well here, served with saffron rice or naan bread. For Vietnamese, Thai, and Asian fusion specialties, head to ★ Uncle Ho's (Calama and Almagro, tel. 2/511-4030, noon-11pm Mon.-Sat., entrées $5-14). Choose from a wide range of tasty rolls, soups, and red and green curries. Weekly fish specials round out the menu showcasing the talent of the kitchen. It's a good place for a drink too, and friendly Scottish owner Stewart is usually behind the bar keeping the party going. Uncle Ho's doubles as the expat hangout and is a good place to find solid information about travel in Ecuador if stuck.

Cafés, Bakeries, and Snacks

El Cafécito (Cordero 1124 at Reina Victoria, tel. 2/223-4862, entrées $3-8) is a good option for breakfast as well as Italian and Mexican dishes later on. Candles and crayons for coloring your place mat and a fireplace add to the cozy ambience. The Magic Bean (Foch 681 at Juan León Mera, tel. 2/256-6181, 7am-11pm daily) is another great option for breakfast with fresh Colombian coffee, crepes, and a wide range of juices. Cafe Spiral (Mallorca N24-266 between Coruña and Guipuzcoa, tel. 2/222-7770, 9am-10pm Mon.-Thurs., 9am-midnight

Uncle Ho's

Fri.-Sat., $4-10) is a charming expat-run café in a renovated house with an ample selection of pastries, breakfast fare, sandwiches and soups, paninis and salads. The owners plan to develop it into a cultural center and donate a percentage of their profits to a different nonprofit every month.

Another good option for breakfasts and snacks is El Español (Juan León Mera and Wilson, tel. 2/255-3995, 8am-9pm Mon.-Fri., 8am-6pm Sat.-Sun., entrées $3-6), a chain delicatessen with great sandwiches and high-quality cured hams and cheeses.

Chocoholics should head to Kallari Café (Wilson E4-266 and Juan Leon Mera, tel. 2/223-6009, www.kallari.com, 9am-5pm daily, hours vary so call ahead, $3-8), a community-run café showcasing chocolate and coffee from a collective of growers. They also have cheap but tasty breakfast and lunch fare.

The Coffee Academy (J. Carrión y Juan León Mera, tel. 2/252-7361, 8am-8pm Mon.-Fri., $3-10) is a small, independent, espresso bar 10 minutes from Plaza Foch. They feature organically grown coffee from their family's plantation a few hours away in Puerto Quito. They also hold monthly language exchanges, when the café stays open until 10pm.

Burgers and Steaks

Burgers, grilled plates, and barbecue are the specialties at Adam's Rib (La Niña and Reina Victoria, tel. 2/256-3196, noon-11pm Mon.-Sat., $6-12). For aged Argentinian beef try La Casa de Mi Abuela (Juan Leon Mera 1649 and La Niña, tel. 2/256-5667, noon-11pm Mon.-Sat., $4-7), a Quito institution in the renovated house of the owner's grandmother. While known for its Asian fare, Uncle Ho's (Almagro and Calama, 2/511-4030, noon-11pm Mon.-Sat., entrées $8-12) has one of Quito's best steaks on the menu. On Monday try their weekly steak and mash special for the price of a regular entrée.

For arguably the best burgers and wings in town, head to King's Cross Bar (La Niña and Reina Victoria, tel. 2/255-3132, 6pm-midnight Mon.-Thurs., 5:30pm til as late as 2:30am Fri.-Sat., $5-8) where the Ecuadorian/Canadian owner has been dishing up her two menu items while tending bar amidst the city's trendsetters for twenty years.

Cuban

The cuisine of this Caribbean island has become quite popular in Ecuador. There are two good places at the north end of Mariscal. Varadero Sandwiches Cubanos (Reina

Cafe Spiral

Victoria and La Pinta, tel. 2/254-2757, noon-4pm and 7pm-midnight Mon.-Sat., entrées $5) has sandwiches, and things heat up at night with live music by the bar. La Bodeguita de Cuba (Reina Victoria 1721 at La Pinta, tel. 2/254-2476, noon-4pm and 7pm-midnight Mon.-Sat., entrées $4-6) is popular for its Cuban *bocaditos* (appetizers) as well as the live Cuban music on Thursday nights.

Ecuadorian

Amidst the dozens of international restaurants, a few eateries offering local specialties stand out. La Choza (12 de Octubre 1821 at Cordero, tel. 2/223-0839, noon-4pm and 7pm-10pm Mon.-Fri., noon-4pm Sat.-Sun., $3-20) is a popular mid-price place serving appetizers such as *tortillas de maíz* and entrées like the tasty *locro de papas*. For larger portions, try Mama Clorinda (Reina Victoria 1144 at Calama, tel. 2/254-4362, 11am-10pm Mon.-Sat.), where you can get *llapingachos* and a quarter of a chicken for $6, or try a half guinea pig (*cuy*) for $10.

French

Gallic cuisine tends to be served in the most upscale of Quito's foreign restaurants. Le Petit Pigalle (9 de Octubre y Carrion, tel. 2/252-0867, www.lepetitpigallerestaurant. com, 12:30pm-3pm and 5pm-11pm Mon.-Fri., 1:30pm-4pm Sat., entrées $15-30) is among the best restaurants in the city. Make reservations and dress well. Born from owners Cristina Carranco and Johan Ducroquet's experience in fine-dining restaurants in Paris and Lasarte-Oria, classic French food dominates the menu with an excellent selection of French, Spanish, and Argentinian wines to accompany every plate.

For a more economical dip into French fare, La Crêpes de Paris (Calama E7-62 y Diego de Almagro, tel. 9/400-0480, 12:30pm-11pm Weds.-Sat., entrées $4-8) has a small menu of sweet and savory crepes, French onion soup, and a croque monsieur sandwich.

Italian

As the city has spread north, several classy restaurants have followed the business-lunch crowd up Eloy Alfaro. One of the best, Sol y Luna (Whymper N 31-29 y Coruña, tel. 2/223-5865, 12:30pm-3:30pm and 7pm-11pm Mon.-Sat., entrées $7-16), has a generous selection of traditional dishes including carpaccio, pasta, gnocchi, fish, and desserts. Good service and generous portions make the prices more bearable, as does the delicious tiramisu. For more economical pizza and pasta, try Le Arcate (Baquedano 358 at Juan León Mera, lunch and dinner daily, entrées $6-14), which offers over 50 varieties of wood-oven pizzas (the "Russian" has vodka as an ingredient) for $6-9. An expat favorite is Cosa Nostra Trattoría Pizzería (Moreno and Almagro, tel. 2/252-7145, noon-3pm and 6:30pm-11pm Mon.-Sat., entrées $6-14) has a substantial selection of pizza, spaghetti, ravioli, and gnocchi. The owner, Simone, is from Italy and not only brought his family recipes to Quito but their hospitality as well. Check the chalkboard for weekly specials. Located close to Parque Carolina Romolo e Remo (Av. Republica del Salvador N34-399, tel. 2/600-0683, 9am-8pm Mon.-Sat., entrées $2.50-10) has a small, inexpensive menu of pizzas, pastas, and focaccia using imported ingredients, which are also for sale. The house gnocchi is rich beyond measure, combining homemade tomato sauce, flavorful cheese, and fresh basil into a scrumptious dish.

Mexican

A plate of fajitas at Red Hot Chili Peppers (Foch and Juan León Mera, tel. 2/255-7575, noon-11pm Mon.-Sat., entrées $5-8) will easily fill two people. A tiny place with a big TV and graffiti covering the walls, it serves the best Tex-Mex food (and the best margaritas) in town. A pricier option located North of the Mariscal in the El Batan Alto neighborhood, La Vecindad de Los Cuates (Guanguiltagua n3997 y Tomas Belmur, tel. 2/246-5053, noon-4:30pm Mon., noon-11pm

Tues.-Fri., 12:30pm-4:30pm and 6:30pm-11pm Sat.) is worth seeking out for the big plates of authentic Mexican food despite its out-of-the-way location on the border of Parque Metropolitano.

Middle Eastern

Shawarma (grilled meat in warm pita bread with yogurt sauce and vegetables) is becoming more and more popular in Ecuador, and Middle Eastern restaurants are springing up left, right, and center. In Mariscal, El Arabe (Reina Victoria 627 at Carrión, tel. 2/254-9414, 10am-9pm Mon.-Sat., 11am-7pm Sun., entrées $6-8) is a long-established popular spot. The patio at Aladdin (Almagro and Baquerizo Moreno, tel. 2/222-9435, 10:30am-midnight daily, entrées $2-4) is always packed at night. The water pipes and 16 kinds of flavored tobacco probably have something to do with it, along with the cheap falafel and *shawarma*.

Baalbek (Av. 6 de Diciembre N23-103 y Wilson, tel. 2/255-2766, noon-5pm and 7pm-10:30pm Weds.-Fri., noon-5pm Sat.-Tue., entrées $6-14) stands out for its small plates including hummus, *mansafh, fatush* and other Lebanese favorites. Go on Thursday night for the weekly belly-dancing show.

Seafood

Two restaurants stand out in this category: Mare Nostrum (Tamayo 172 at Foch, tel. 2/252-8686, noon-10pm Tues.-Sat., entrées $8-17) claims to have "70 ways of serving fish." Boat models, suits of armor, low lighting, and dark wood beams in a castle-like building set the stage for delicious cream soups and *encocados* served in half a coconut shell. For *ceviche,* Cevicheria Manolo (Diego de Almagro 1170 y La Niña, tel. 2/256-9294,

9am-5pm Mon.-Sat., $7-12) is a favorite with a wide selection of Ecuadorian and Peruvian ceviches.

Vegetarian

Being vegetarian tends to attract quizzical looks around Ecuador, but in Quito there are several good options. El Maple (Pinto E7-68 and Almagro, tel. 2/290-0000, noon-9pm daily, entrées $3-5) has everything from pasta and curry to burritos and stir-fries. Lunch is a great value at $4.50.

Formosa (Jeronimo Carrion y Juan Leon Mera, tel. 8/340-4667, 10am-4pm daily, entrées $3-7) is a favorite of vegetarians for its Taiwanese vegan and veggie food and set lunch specials.

Other International

For a tangy Swiss fondue, try La Maison du Fromage (Av. Eloy Alfaro N32-656 y Rusia, tel. 2/227-5938, lunch and dinner Mon.-Sat., entrées $6-12), which also sells the artisanal cheeses and wines it serves in the restaurant. La Paella Valenciana (Republica and Almagro, tel. 2/222-8681, noon-3pm and 7:30pm-11:30pm Mon.-Sat., noon-3pm Sun., entrées $10-20) is one of the best places for a wide range of Spanish entrées and tapas.

One of the most enticing restaurants in Mariscal is the colorful, glass-encased patio of ★ La Boca del Lobo (Calama 284 at Reina Victoria, tel. 2/254-5500, 5pm-midnight Mon.-Sat., entrées $7-14). The decor is flamboyantly eclectic, with birdcages and psychedelic paintings, and the menu focuses on Mediterranean specialties—marvel at how many ways they can cook mushrooms. The cocktail menu is another highlight. This place attracts a higher-class crowd and is also gay friendly.

Information and Services

VISITOR INFORMATION

The Corporación Metropolitana de Turismo (Quito Visitors Bureau) is the best tourist information bureau in Ecuador and an excellent source of information on Quito, with maps, brochures, leaflets, English-speaking staff, and a regularly updated website. The main office is at the Palacio Municipal (Plaza de la Independencia, Venezuela and Espejo, tel. 2/257-2445, 9am-6pm Mon.-Fri., 9am-5pm Sat.). There are also branches in Mariscal (Reina Victoria and Luis Cordero, tel. 2/255-1566), the airport (tel. 2/330-0164), the Museo Nacional del Banco Central (6 de Diciembre and Patria, tel. 2/222-1116), and at Quitumbe bus terminal.

The Quito Visitors Bureau works with the Tourism Unit of the Metropolitan Police (tel. 2/257-0786) to provide guided tours of the city. These well-informed officers are clad in blue-and-red uniforms (and look rather like airline pilots). Tours of Old Town range $6-15 pp, and a tour of Mitad del Mundo costs $40.

The main office of Ecuador's Ministerio de Turismo (Eloy Alfaro N32-300 at Tobar, 3rd Fl., tel. 2/239-9333, 8:30am-12:30pm and 1:30pm-5pm daily), near the Parque La Carolina, is also helpful and can assist with hotel reservations. It has maps, and some staff speak English.

VISAS

Tourist-visa extensions beyond the standard 90 days are the main reason most travelers end up at the Ministerio de Relaciones Exteriores (Carrión E1-76 at 10 de Agosto, tel. 2/299-3200, www.mmrree.gob.ec, 8:30am-1:30pm Mon.-Fri.). Go early and be ready to wait. All nontourist visa holders (student, cultural, volunteer, or work visas) must register within 30 days of arrival at the same office; otherwise you have to pay a $200 fine.

EMBASSIES AND CONSULATES

The following nations have embassies or consulates in Quito: Canada (Amazonas 4153 at Unión Nacional de Periodistas, tel. 2/245-5499, 9am-noon and 2:30pm-5:30pm Mon.-Fri., appointment required, Australians also welcome; the Australian consulate is in Guayaquil); Colombia (consulate: Atahualpa 955 at República, 3rd Fl., tel. 2/245-8012, 8:30am-1pm Mon.-Fri; embassy: Colón 1133 at Amazonas, Ed. Arist, 7th Fl., tel. 2/222-8926, 9am-1pm and 2pm-4pm Mon.-Fri.); Peru (República de El Salvador 495 at Irlanda, tel. 2/246-8410, 9am-1pm and 3pm-5pm Mon.-Fri.); United Kingdom (Ed. Citiplaza, 14th Fl., Naciones Unidas and República de El Salvador, tel. 2/297-0800, http://ukinecuador.fco.gov.uk, 8:30am-12:30pm and 1:30pm-5pm Mon.-Thurs., 8:30am-1:30pm Fri.); and the United States (Avigiras and Guayacanes, tel. 2/398-5000, http://ecuador.usembassy.gov, 8am-12:30pm and 1:30pm-5pm Tues.-Fri.).

MAPS

The hike up Paz y Miño is worth it for the commanding view of the city from the Instituto Geográfico Militar (IGM, tel. 2/250-2091, 8am-4pm Mon.-Fri.). Here you can get general tourist maps of Ecuador, as well as topographical maps for hiking. While you wait for the staff to process your map order (bring a book), consider a show at the planetarium. The IGM often closes early on Fridays, and visitors must surrender their passports at the gate to enter.

The Quito Visitors Bureau (Plaza de la Independencia, Venezuela and Espejo, tel. 2/257-2445, 9am-6pm Mon.-Fri., 9am-5pm Sat.) can supply decent maps for visitors as well as specialist walking tour maps.

Emergency Phone Numbers

- Police — 101
- Fire Department — 102
- Red Cross — 131
- Emergency — 911

POST OFFICES AND COURIERS

Quito's main post office is in New Town (Eloy Alfaro 354 at 9 de Octubre, tel. 2/256-1218, 8am-6pm Mon.-Fri., 8am-noon Sat.). The Express Mail Service (EMS, tel. 2/256-1962) is at this office. There is also a branch post office one block east of the Plaza de la Independencia in Old Town (Espejo between Guayaquil and Venezuela, tel. 2/228-2175, 8am-6pm Mon.-Fri.).

If you're sending something important, using an international courier service is preferable. There is a branch of FedEx (Amazonas 517 at Santa María, tel. 2/227-9180), and DHL has several offices throughout the city, including on Eloy Alfaro and Avenida de Los Juncos (tel. 2/397-5000), Colón 1333 at Foch (tel. 2/255-6118), at the Hilton Colón, and at the airport.

TELECOMMUNICATIONS

Telephone

You're never far from a *cabina* offering telephone service. The national companies Andinatel and Pacifictel no longer have a monopoly—together with Claro (Porta), Movistar, and Alegro, they both run competing offices. Movistar and Claro also have pay phones everywhere, and each type requires its own brand of prepaid card. The most convenient offices in Mariscal are at Juan León Mera 741 at Baquedano, and on Reina Victoria near Calama.

Internet Access

Internet access is even easier to find than a phone booth. Internet cafés are everywhere, particularly in Mariscal. Expect to pay $1 per hour and to have access at most cafés 8am-9pm daily, possibly later on weekends. Although connection rates and computer quality vary widely, most cafés have fax service, scanners, printers, and Internet phone programs, allowing foreign visitors to call home for a fraction of the cost of a regular phone connection. The term *café* may be misleading, however, because many offer only water and snacks.

Listing Internet cafés in Quito is an inherently futile gesture because they open and close so fast. In New Town, the block of Calama between Juan León Mera and Reina Victoria has a handful. The increasing number of hotels with free Internet access and Wi-Fi often makes a visit to an Internet café unnecessary.

MONEY

Banks and ATMs

ATMs for most international systems (Plus, Cirrus, Visa, and MasterCard) can be found at major banks along Amazonas and around the shopping centers. These tend to have limits on how much you can withdraw per day (usually $300), so if you need to, say, pay cash for a Galápagos trip, you'll have to go to a bank branch. It's best to take a taxi straight to the travel agency if you withdraw a large amount of money. Banco del Pacífico has its head office on Naciones Unidos at Los Shyris, and there is a branch at Amazonas and Washington. Banco de Guayaquil is on Reina Victoria at Colón, and on Amazonas at Veintimilla; Banco de Pichincha is on Amazonas at Pereira, and on 6 de Diciembre. Banco Bolivariano is at Naciones Unidas E6-99.

Exchange Houses

Since the introduction of the U.S. dollar, exchanging other currencies has become more difficult, and many exchange houses have closed. Try to bring U.S. dollars travelers checks, as rates are poor for Canadian dollars, British pounds, and even the euro. Exchanging those currencies outside Quito, Guayaquil, and Cuenca is difficult if not impossible. If you really have to, try one of the large banks listed above.

Credit Card Offices

Visa (Los Shyris 3147, tel. 2/245-9303) has an office in Quito, as do American Express (Ed. Rocafuerte, 5th Fl., Amazonas 339 at Jorge Washington, tel. 2/256-0488) and MasterCard (Naciones Unidas and Shyris, tel. 2/226-2770).

Money Transfers

Western Union (8am-6pm Mon.-Fri., 9am-5pm Sat.-Sun.) has many locations around the city, including on Av. Del República and on Colón—check www.westernunion.com for a list of offices worldwide. The company charges $52 for a same-day transfer of $1,000, plus local taxes. It'll cost you $25 to transfer any amount to and from other places in the Americas, and $35 to and from Europe, at the Banco del Pacífico (Amazonas and Jorge Washington); you are also expected to cover the cost of contacting your home bank. If that much cash makes you itch, you can change it into American Express travelers checks at the main branch of the Banco del Pacífico (República 433 at Almagro). This transaction costs $10 to change up to $1,000, and 1 percent of the total for additional amounts.

HEALTH
General Concerns

Unless you're traveling from an equally high city such as La Paz, you will certainly feel the effects of Quito's elevation within the first few hours of arriving. At best, you will feel a bit breathless and light-headed, but dizzy spells, headaches, and fatigue are also common. It is best not to overexert yourself, to minimize caffeine and alcohol intake, and consume plenty of water and light food. After

two or three days, you'll more or less be used to the elevation.

Don't let the cool climate at this elevation fool you into thinking that you don't need to bother with sunblock. The sun is far stronger up here, so slap it on. The smog from the traffic can leave you with a sore throat, particularly because Quito's location in a valley seems to trap all the pollution.

Like everywhere in Ecuador, you may suffer from stomach problems. Minimize the risks by avoiding salad, unpeeled fruit, ice, pork, and shellfish. Don't eat on the street or from bus vendors.

Hospitals and Clinics

The Hospital Metropolitano (Mariana de Jesús and Occidental, tel. 2/226-1520) is the best hospital in Quito and is priced accordingly. The American-run Hospital Voz Andes (Villalengua 267 at 10 de Agosto, tel. 2/226-2142) is cheaper and receives the most business from Quito's foreign residents. It's described as fast, competent, and inexpensive, with an emergency room and outpatient services. To get there, take the *trole* north along 10 de Agosto just past Naciones Unidas.

The 24-hour Clínica Pichincha (Veintimilla E3-30 at Páez, tel. 2/299-8700) has a laboratory that can perform analyses for intestinal parasites. Women's health problems should be referred to the 24-hour Clínica de la Mujer (Amazonas N39-216 at Gaspar de Villarroel, tel. 2/245-8000).

OTHER SERVICES
Laundry

Wash-and-dry places are common in New Town: There are several on Foch, Pinto, and Wilson between Reina Victoria and Amazonas. A few may even let you use the machines yourself. Laundry services are available in many hotels, and the receptionists in more expensive ones can point you toward a dry cleaner (*lavaseca*).

Quito City Discover Card

For those in Quito for at least a week, the

Quito City Discover Card ($15, valid for 15 days) gives substantial discounts at many of the museums and restaurants around Quito. For a list of discounts and to buy a card online, visit www.quitocitydiscover.com.

Spanish Lessons

Ecuador is quickly becoming one of the best places to learn Spanish in Latin America. Not only do Ecuadorians—at least those who live in the mountains—speak slowly and clearly in comparison to their quick-talking, slang-tossing neighbors, but competition among dozens of schools keeps prices low and quality up—and it's a great place to travel.

Dozens of schools in Quito offer intensive Spanish instruction, and it's worth your while to shop around for one that fits your needs perfectly. Tuition usually includes 2-6 hours of instruction per day, either in groups or one-on-one (four hours daily is usually plenty). Costs range $6-12 per hour. An initial registration fee may be required, and discounts are often possible for long-term commitments. Make sure to get a receipt when you pay, and check to see if any extras are not included in the hourly rate.

Many schools draw business by offering extras such as sports facilities and extracurricular activities. Some will house you (for a fee) or arrange for a homestay with a local family (typically $10-25 per day for full board, $9-15 for lodging only). Don't sign any long-term arrangements until you're sure of both the school and the family.

The following schools have received many positive reviews:

- **The Experiment in International Living** (Hernando de la Cruz N31-37 y Mariana de Jesús, tel. 2/255-1937,www.ei-lecuador.org)

- **Yanapuma Spanish School** (Guayaquil N9-59 y Oriente, tel. 2/228-0843,www.yanapumaspanish.org)

- **Cristóbal Colón Spanish School** (Colón 2088 at Versalles, tel./fax 2/250-6508, www.colonspanishschool.com)

- **Guayasamín Spanish School** (Calama E8-54 near 6 de Diciembre, tel. 2/254-4210, www.guayasaminschool.com)

- **Instituto Superior de Español** (Darquea Terán 1650 at 10 de Agosto, tel. 2/222-3242, www.instituto-superior.net)

- **La Lengua** (Ed. Ave María, 8th Fl., Colón 1001 at Juan León Mera, tel./fax 2/250-1271, www.la-lengua.com)

- **South American Language Center** (Amazonas N26-59 at Santa María, tel. 2/254-4715, www.southamerican.edu.ec)

Getting There and Around

GETTING THERE AND AWAY
Air

After seven years of construction and a cost of more than $500 million, Mariscal Sucre International Airport (tel. 395-4200, www.aeropuertoquito.aero) opened in February of 2013. The new facility replaced the old airport of the same name and services all airlines flying in and out of Quito.

The new facility is located in the suburb of Tababela, 12 kilometers east of Quito's center. The route from Quito isn't direct (it's about 23 km of roadway), and travel times vary depending on traffic. A good rule of thumb is to allow two hours during peak time and one in the early morning and late evening.

Taxis are arranged at the clearly marked desk next to the Thrifty, Hertz, Avis, Budget, and Localiza car rental booths. Taxis to and from the airport have set rates from $25 to $50 corresponding to the different areas of the city. Set rates by zone are posted at the taxi desk at the airport. The normal rate for either the Mariscal or the Old Town is $25 each way. If charged more than the set rate, you may file a complaint with the National Police as a third-class traffic violation, deserving of a 15 percent minimum wage fine and a four and a half point loss on the driver's license. Knowing this fact can be useful when bartering for a price.

Aeroservicios (http://aeroservicios.com.ec) offers an airport shuttle running between the old and new airport for $8. The buses run 'round the clock and depart every 30 minutes. Buses have free Wi-Fi, and passengers are allowed one bag up to 50 lbs. and a small carry-on bag. A $2 fee is charged for each additional bag. Tickets can be bought at each location with cash or credit card or online.

Public transportation between the airport and the Northern Río Coca bus terminal runs until 10 p.m. for $2. The bus route contains 11 stops, so add additional time to travel if choosing this option. Be aware of pickpockets and that during peak hours there is no such thing as personal space.

Airport services include 60 check-in counters, self-service check-in kiosks, tourist information, a post office, a few fast food restaurants and coffee stands, a money exchange, ATMs, airport shuttles, duty-free shops, Wi-Fi, a VIP lounge, and expedited check-in assistance. Personalized arrival and departure assistance and access to the VIP lounge ($20) are arranged through the airport's customer service collections office (Level 1 of the Passenger Terminal, next to the Administrative Entrance and Amazonía Café, 2/294-4900 ext. 2618, servicio.cliente@quiport.com).

Choices for places to stay nearby are few but growing with the airport's opening. Quito Airport Suites (971 Alfonso Tobar y Tulio Garzon, tel. 2/239-1430, http://airporthotelquito.com, $49 s, $55 d) offers airport pickup, luggage storage, free breakfast, and the usual amenities found at airport hotels.

AIRLINES IN QUITO

TAME (Amazonas 13-54 at Colón, tel. 2/290-9900 or 700/500-800) has flights from Quito to Baltra in the Galápagos ($450-620 round-trip) and to the following destinations for $50-90 one-way: Coca, Cuenca, Esmeraldas, Guayaquil, Lago Agrio, Loja, Machala, and Tulcán. Icaro (Palora 124 at Amazonas, tel. 2/245-0928) is sometimes marginally cheaper and has daily flights to Coca, Cuenca, Manta, and Guayaquil. Aerogal (Amazonas 607 y Carrión, tel. 2/255-3248) flies to Guayaquil and the Galápagos and also has daily flights to Cuenca. SAEREO (Indanza 121 at Amazonas, tel. 2/330-1152) has a daily flight to Macas.

The following airlines also serve Quito: Air France and KLM (12 de Octubre N 26-27 at A. Lincoln, Edificio Torre 1492, of. 1103, tel. 2/396-6728, shared offices); American Airlines (Av. de los Shyris N35-174 at Suecia Edif. Renazzo Plaza, Planta Baja, tel. 2/299-5000); Avianca (Coruña 1311 at San Ignacio, tel. 2/255-6715); Copa República de El Salvador 361 at Moscu, tel. 2/227-3082); Delta (Ed. Renazzo Plaza, 3rd Fl., Los Shyris and Suecia, tel. 2/333-1691); Iberia (Ed. Finandes, Eloy Alfaro 939 at Amazonas, tel. 2/256-6009); Japan Airlines (Amazonas 3899 at Corea, tel. 2/298-6828); Lan (Amazonas and Pasaje Guayas, tel. 2/255-1782); Lufthansa (Ed. Harmonia, Amazonas N47-205 at Río Palora, tel. 2/226-7705); Taca (República de El Salvador N34-67 at Suecia, tel. 800/008-222); United Airlines (12 de Octubre at Cordero, Edificio World Trade Center, Torre B, tel. 2/255-7290).

International Buses

Rutas de America (Selva Alegre OE-72 y Av. 10 de Agosto, tel. 2/254-8142 or 2/250-3611, www.rutasamerica.com) offers direct service to and from Peru and Columbia and is considered one of the most trustworthy international bus companies. Buses come from Peru, so one must call to find out exactly when they will

Buses from Quito Terminals

FROM QUITUMBE

Ambato	$2.70	2.5 hours
Atacames	$8	7 hours
Baños	$3.70	3 hours
Coca	$10	9 hours
Cuenca	$12	9 hours
Esmeraldas	$7	6 hours
Guaranda	$4.50	5 hours
Guayaquil	$8	8 hours
Lago Agrio	$8	9 hours
Latacunga	$1.70	1.5 hours
Macas	$8	7 hours
Puyo	$5	5 hours
Santo Domingo	$3	3 hours
Tena	$6	5 hours

FROM CARCELÉN

Atacames	$8	7 hours
Esmeraldas	$7	6 hours
Ibarra	$2.50	2.5 hours
Los Bancos	$2.50	2 hours (indirect to Mindo)
Otavalo	$2.50	2 hours
Tulcán	$5	5 hours

FROM OFELIA

Cayambe	$1.50	1.5 hours
Mindo (direct)	$2.50	2 hours
Mitad del Mundo	$0.40	1.5 hours (via the Metrobus line)

arrive in Quito. Buses depart for Columbia on Mondays, Wednesdays, and Saturdays around midnight. Buses to Lima leave on Thursdays at 3am and Sundays at 11pm. The company often posts new routes and the arrival times in Quito on their Facebook page.

Expreso Internacional Ormeño (Av. Los Shyris 34432 y Portugal, tel. 2/214-0487, www.grupo-ormeno.com.pe) offers daily buses to Lima and Columbia. For a complete list, check http://andestransit.com.

National Buses

Quito has replaced its dilapidated old bus station at Cumandá with three different terminals. The biggest terminal, Quitumbe, in the far south of Quito, is a joy to visit; security and cleanliness are both excellent. This terminal serves all long-distance routes traveling west, east, and south as well as services to the north to Esmeraldas via Santo Domingo. Those traveling to other destinations north and northwest need to head for either the Carcelén terminal or La Ofelia terminal, both in the far north of Quito. Trole, Ecovia, and Metrobus have extended their services to all three main bus terminals, running until midnight on weekdays and until 10pm on weekends.

Buses leave every 20 minutes from 5am until 8pm from the North terminal (Carcelén) and the South terminal (Quitumbe) to Otavalo and Baños, respectively. La Ofelia is the only terminal that offers direct service to Mindo, with five buses departing for Mindo during the week (8am, 9am, 11am, 1pm, 4pm).

Generally, bus company's websites in

Ecuador are not maintained as well as those in other Latin American countries and shouldn't be trusted. For the most accurate online schedule for most destinations in Ecuador, check www.ecuadorschedules.com as it is updated regularly.

The northern terminal at Ofelia, which is only for county buses, is where Coop Pichincha serves Guayllabamba and El Quinche; San José de Minas serves the northwest (Nanegal, Minas, Chontal, Cielo Verde); Flor de Valle goes to Cayambe, Pacto, and Mindo; Transportes Otavalo serves Minas and Pacto; and Malchingui and Cangahua run buses to various locations. Ofelia is the end of the Metrovia city bus route, and dozens of connections spread out from here into the northern parishes. The terminal is clean, organized, and well signposted. The Mitad del Mundo buses come through here—use your existing bus ticket and pay just $0.15 extra for the transfer.

Rental Cars and Motorcycles

Renting a car may be a good way to get out of the city, but take into account the convenience and cheapness of buses as well as the many vagaries of driving in Ecuador. It's definitely not the way to see the city.

Small cars start at $50 per day. Several major car-rental companies operate in Quito, including Avis (at the airport, tel. 2/281-8160, www.avis.com.ec); Thrifty (at the airport, tel. 2/281-8160, www.thrifty.com.ec); Budget (Av. Eloy Alfaro S 40-153 and José Queri, tel. 2/224-4095, www.budget-ec.com); and Hertz (at the airport, tel. 2/281-8410, www.hertz.com).

Other options include Safari Tours (Av. Del Establo 181 and Las Garzas, Cumbaya, tel. 2/255-2505, www.safari.com.ec), which has some 4WD vehicles and drivers available to head into the mountains, and it can arrange larger cars and buses for groups. Ecuadorian Alpine Institute (Ramírez Dávalos 136 at Amazonas, Suite 102, tel. 2/256-5465, fax 2/256-8949, eai@ecuadorexplorer.com, www.

volcanoclimbing.com) has 4WD vehicles as well.

For motorcycles, American-owned Ecuador Freedom Bike Rental (Juan León Mera N22-37 at Veintimilla, tel. 2/250-4339, www.freedombikerental.com) offers several different options for exploring the country on their growing fleet of high-end motorcycles and scooters. These include guided tours and self-guided GPS tours through the Andes, the coast, and the jungle using relatively unknown routes. Safety equipment is provided.

Trains

Quito's Chimbacalle train station (Sincholagua and Maldonado) is a few kilometers south of Old Town. The trolley is the easiest way to reach it, and the Chimbacalle stop is right at the station, which is a delightful step back in time.

At present there are services from Quito to Boliche (Thurs.-Sun., 8 hours, $25 round-trip), Machachi (Thurs.-Sun., 8 hours, $20 round-trip), and Latacunga (Thurs.-Sun., 10 hours, $20 round-trip). There is a new route from Quito to Durán outside of Guayaquil that takes three nights and four days to complete. Trains leave twice a month and the cost including hotels is $1,270 (www.ecuadorbytrain.com).

GETTING AROUND
Local Buses

If you're traveling a relatively simple route, local buses can be useful. The routes are rather complicated, so it's best to take short journeys along the major roads, especially Amazonas and 10 de Agosto. It's a good idea to ask a local at the bus stop which bus number goes to your destination. For more complex journeys, you're better off taking the trolley systems or a taxi.

Any of 10 de Agosto's major crossroads, including Patria, Orellana, and Naciones Unidas, are likely places to find a bus heading south to Old Town or north as far as the turn to Mitad del Mundo. "La Y," the meeting of 10 de Agosto with América and De la Prensa, is a major bus intersection, as is Parque Huayna Capac at 6 de Diciembre and El Inca. The flat fare is $0.25. Have it ready, and take care with your belongings on crowded buses.

Trolley Systems

Quito's network of three electric trolley buses is the best of its kind in Ecuador: It is cheap, clean, fast, and well-organized. The buses are separated from ordinary traffic to avoid delays. Flat fare for all services is $0.25, payable at kiosks or machines on entry. Cars pass every 5-10 minutes.

El Trole (5:30am-11:30pm Mon.-Fri., 6am-10pm Sat.-Sun.) runs north-south from Estación Norte north of New Town near La Y, south past stops at Mariscal and Colón, through Old Town past Chimbacalle train station, to the new southern bus terminal at Quitumbe. It takes about an hour to get to Quitumbe from New Town. The main *trole* thoroughfare, 10 de Agosto, reserves a pair of center lanes for the service, detouring down Guayaquil and Maldonado in Old Town, then continuing on Maldonado south of El Panecillo.

The **Ecovia** (6am-10pm Mon.-Fri., 6am-9pm Sat.-Sun.) is similar, but without the overhead wires. It also runs north-south from its northern Río Coca terminal along 6 de Diciembre past La Casa de la Cultura to La Marín near Old Town. Most trolleys turn around at La Marín, where there are interchanges with many country bus routes to the south and the valley; an extension continues past the exit of the old Cumandá bus terminal to Avenida Napo.

The third line, called **Metrobus** (5:30am-10:30pm Mon.-Fri., 6am-10pm Sat.-Sun.), runs from La Marín in Old Town up Santa Prisca and along Avenida América, La Prensa, and north to both the Ofelia and Carcelén terminals, where there are connections to the northern highlands, cloud forest, and northern coast. It takes about 40 minutes to get to these terminals from New Town.

If you want to bypass Quito by traveling between Carcelén in the north and Quitumbe in the south, there is now a direct shuttle service.

It all seems too good to be true, and in one sense, it is: Unfortunately, all of the trolley lines are notorious for highly skilled **pickpockets,** and foreign visitors are easy targets. If you're going sightseeing with your camera, avoid crowded services and consider taking a taxi. Don't take valuables or large amounts of cash on the bus, and if possible,

The newly opened train route between Quito and Durán is a luxurious way to travel.

avoid traveling at peak times in morning or late-afternoon rush hour.

For further information on the trolley-buses, visit www.trolebus.gov.ec.

Taxis

Digital meters are required in taxis by law. Many drivers will pretend that the meters are out of order ("*no funciona*"), in which case you should offer to find another cab. Saying this has a strange tendency to fix malfunctioning meters instantly, although many drivers will refuse to use them, even though that's illegal. Meters start at $0.35, with a $1 minimum charge, and run except when the cab is stopped. Rides within Old Town and New Town as well as between the two areas shouldn't be more than $2.50 during the day. Prices increase at night, but shouldn't be more than double. Drivers are particularly reluctant to use the meter for longer trips to the bus terminals. Rates tend to vary from $5 to Carcelén and Ofelia to $8 to Quitumbe.

Regulations now require that all licensed taxis in Quito have a red panic button in the back and two cameras installed in the cab. The cameras have tape on them indicating that they haven't been tampered with. If the tape is missing, consider taking another taxi.

Freelance yellow cabs prowl the streets, and various small taxi stands exist all over the city, especially in front of expensive hotels. These have a set price list for destinations and are usually more expensive than a metered ride. Prebooking a taxi from your hotel is by far the best option because the hotelier will use

a reliable company. Otherwise, never take an unmarked cab, and in the case of yellow taxis, check for the orange license plate as well as the company name and registration on the side of the cab and on the windshield. The driver should also have an ID. Don't be afraid to ask for this ("*identidad*") before getting in. All these precautions will minimize the risk of being a victim of crime, which has become more common in Quito taxis in recent years.

Radio taxis can be called at a moment's notice or arranged the day before. Try the Central de Radio Taxi (tel. 2/250-0600 or 2/252-1112) or Taxi Amigo (tel. 2/222-2222 or 2/222-2220). Both are reliable and available at any hour. Taxis Lagos de Ibarra (Asunción 381 at Versalles, tel. 2/256-5992) sends five-passenger taxis to Ibarra for $9 pp, or to Otavalo for $8 pp. Sudamericana Taxis (tel. 2/275-2567) sends cabs to Santo Domingo or stops along the way, such as La Hesperia or Tinalandia, for $15 pp.

Bicycles

BiciQ (Joaquín Pinto Oe4-130 y Luis Cordero, tel. 2/395-2300, biciq@quito.gob.ec, www.biciq.gob.ec, 7am-7pm daily) has public bicycles available for 45 minutes at many stations located throughout the city. Registration can be done online or at the main office. The service costs $25 a year but is a worthwhile expense if you are in Quito for a few days. Processing time takes 72 hours, so sign up before you arrive. Although the 45-minute timeframe is short, you can pick up another bike immediately after dropping the last one off.

Vicinity of Quito

CALDERÓN

Just nine kilometers from Quito's northern suburbs, artisans in this tiny town craft figures out of a varnished bread dough called *masapan*. This technique, unique to Ecuador until Play-Doh came along, originated with the annual making of bread babies for Day of the Dead celebrations in November. Artisans in Calderón developed more elaborate and lasting figures, adding salt and carpenter's glue, and the villagers gradually created new techniques. With the introduction of aniline dyes, the *masa* became colored.

Today, Calderón is filled with artisan's shops and private houses that turn out the figurines by the hundreds. Tiny indigenous dolls called *cholas* stand in formation on tables and shelves next to brightly painted parrots, llamas, fish, and flowers. Each flour-paste figure is molded by hand or rolled and cut with a pasta maker and pastry cutter. They are then dried, painted, and varnished. The figures make unusual, inexpensive gifts and are popular as Christmas ornaments. Models of Nativity scenes, Santa Claus figures, and decorated trees are sold along the main street. Buses for Calderón leave regularly from the Ofelia terminal.

GUAYLLABAMBA AND VICINITY

Past Calderón, on the road to Cayambe and Otavalo, this small town on the river of the same name is home to the best zoo in the country.

Quito Zoo (tel. 2/236-8898, www.quito-zoo.org, 8:30am-4pm Tues.-Fri., 9am-4pm Sat.-Sun., $4.50), which opened in 1997, is now considered one of the most spacious zoos in Latin America. The largest collection of native fauna in the country occupies the 12-hectare spread, including several animals rescued from the illegal fur trade. The focus is on mammals such as spectacled bears, wolves, monkeys, and pumas; this is also your best chance to see the elusive jaguar, so difficult to spot in the wild. Macaws, parrots, eagles, Andean condors, and toucans represent native birds, and a dozen Galápagos tortoises complete the collection. The zoo is three kilometers from the center of town—take a taxi ($2.25), or it's a long 40-minute walk uphill. Tours are available for $5.

El Quinche

Six kilometers away, through the dry, eroded landscape south of Guayllabamba, is the village of El Quinche. The town's ornate church and sanctuary dedicated to the Virgin of Quinche draw crowds of pilgrims from Quito in search of the Virgin's blessing year-round, and especially at processions honoring the Virgin held on November 21. The shrine is thought to grant special protection to truck and taxi drivers. From here, you can follow the road south to Pifo, then west into Quito's valley suburbs and up into the city.

★ MITAD DEL MUNDO

You can't come to a country that's named after the Equator and not stand with a foot in each hemisphere; a visit to "The Middle of the World" complex is the most popular day trip near Quito. La Mitad del Mundo tourism complex (tel. 2/239-5637, 9am-6pm daily) www.mitaddelmundo.com, $3) lies just beyond the village of Pomasqui, 14 kilometers north of the city.

The centerpiece is a 30-meter-high monument topped by a huge brass globe; a bright red line bisecting it provides the backdrop for the obligatory photo. However, whisper it quietly—the real Equator is actually a few hundred meters away.

It costs an extra $3 to go inside the monument, but it's well worth it for the excellent ethnographic museum. Ascend to the top in an elevator for impressive views over the

Vicinity of Quito

To Otavalo
San Jose de Minas

Nanegal

Fuya Fuya ▲

Lagunas de Mojanda

To Puerto Quito

Nanegalito

Maquipucuna Biological Reserve

San Miguel de los Bancos

TANDAYAP A LODGE

PULULAHUA CRATER ★

RUMICUCHO RUINS ★

COCHASOUI PYRAMIDS ★

Tabacundo

Cayambe

MITAD DEL MUNDO AND MUSEO DE SITIO INTIÑAN

Equator

MINDO LINDO

BELLAVISTA RESERVE

Calacalí

San Antonio del Pichincha

Guayllabamba

Cangahua

Nono

Pomasqui

MINDO

Mindo Forest Reserve

OLD NONO RD

Calderón

El Quinche

HOSTERIA SAN JORGE

Rucu Pichincha

MARISCAL SUCRE INTERNATIONAL AIRPORT

Guagua ▲ Pichincha

QUITO

Chiriboga

SEE "QUITO" MAP

Cumbaya

Tumbaco

Pifo

Cerro Ilaló ▲

PANAMERICANA

PERIFERICO

La Unión del Toachi

Sangolquí

Papallacta Pass

To Santo Domingo de los Colorados

Volcán Atacazo ▲

Cutuglagua

Amaguaña

Pintag

To Papallacta and Baeza

Tambillo

Cerro Pasochoa ▲

Pasochoa Protected Forest

Antisana Reserve

Alóag

Aloasí

Machachi

Volcán Corazón ▲

Volcán Rumiñahui ▲

0   5 mi

0   5 km

© AVALON TRAVEL

To Latacunga ↓

To Cotopaxi ↓

surrounding valley, and then descend the stairs through nine floors of colorful exhibitions on a dozen of Ecuador's diverse indigenous cultures, filled with clothing and artwork. Tours are available in English and Spanish.

The rest of the complex has an assortment of attractions, some more interesting than others. The France building is the best, with a well-presented exhibition on the expedition led by Charles Marie de La Condamine to plot the Equator in the mid-18th century. Another highlight is the intricate model of colonial Quito in the Fundación Quito Colonial ($1.50). The three-square-meter model took

almost seven years to build and has labeled streets. Models of Cuenca, Guayaquil, and various old ships are also part of the display. There is also a planetarium with 40-minute presentations in Spanish ($1.50), artwork in the Spain building, and a small exhibition on insects in the Ecuador room. The Heroes del Cenepa monument near the entrance is dedicated to the soldiers killed in border clashes with Peru in 1995.

On the weekend, the square hosts colorful music and dance performances, and it's a very pleasant place to relax over lunch or a snack in the cluster of cafés.

Tourist agencies offer package tours to

Pululahua and Rumicucho. Calimatours (tel. 2/239-4796 or 2/239-4797), with an office inside the Mitad del Mundo complex, has tours leaving 10am-1pm for $8 pp.

To get here, take the Metrobus on Avenida América to the Ofelia terminal and catch the connecting Mitad del Mundo bus.

★ Museo de Sitio Intiñan

If you've come all this way to stand on the Equator, it's a bit of a shock to hear that the Mitad del Mundo complex was built in the wrong place by a few hundred meters. Understandably, this is kept rather quiet, and you could easily miss the excellent Museo de Sitio Intiñan (tel. 2/239-5122, www. museointinan.com.ec, 9:30am-5pm daily, $4). Located about 300 meters east of the Mitad del Mundo complex, its name means "Museum of the Path of the Sun" in Kichwa, and the family that owns and operates it has done a great job with the collection, which includes displays on local plants and indigenous cultures. However, the real reason to come here are the experiments that you are invited to participate in to prove this really is the site of the Equator—flushing water in opposite directions on either side of the line, walking along the line and feeling the strong gravitational

pull on either side, and the nearly impossible task of balancing an egg on the Equator (you get a certificate if you can do it).

Pululahua Crater and Geobotanical Reserve

About five kilometers north of Mitad del Mundo, the 3,200-hectare Pululahua Reserve ($5 pp) sits inside an extinct volcanic crater. Pululahua bubbled with lava thousands of years ago, but these days the main activity is that of farmers who reside in its flat, fertile bottom. The reserve was officially created in 1978 to protect the rich subtropical ecosystem within one of the largest inhabited craters in South America and possibly the world.

Regular buses and taxis take the road from the base of Mitad del Mundo's pedestrian avenue toward the village of Calacalí. Along the way, a dirt lane leaves the road to the right, after the gas station, and climbs to the lip of the crater at Moraspungo. You can also hike to Pululahua up a road between San Antonio de Pichincha and Calacalí, passing the Ventanilla viewpoint; this becomes a path that continues down into the crater.

El Crater (Pululahua, tel. 2/239-8132, from $98 s or d) is a hotel that perches on the edge of the crater. The panoramic view from the

Museo de Sitio Intiñan

Measuring the Earth

By 1735, most people agreed that the earth was round, but another question remained: *how* round was it? Some scientists theorized that the rotation of the earth caused it to bulge outward slightly in the middle, while others found that idea ridiculous. With explorers setting out daily to the far corners of the globe, it became more and more important to determine how much, if any, the earth bulged in the middle, since navigational charts off by a few degrees could send ships hundreds of kilometers in the wrong direction.

To answer the long-standing debate, the French Academy of Sciences organized two expeditions to determine the true shape of the earth. One team headed north to Lapland, as close to the Arctic as possible. The other left for Ecuador on the equator. Each team was tasked with measuring one degree of latitude, about 110 kilometers, in its respective region. If the length of the degree at the equator proved longer than the degree near the Arctic, then the earth bulged. If they were the same length, it didn't.

The Ecuadorian expedition was the first organized scientific expedition to South America. At the time, Ecuador was part of the Spanish territory of Upper Peru. It was chosen because of its accessibility—much easier to visit than alternate locations along the equator in the Amazon basin, Africa, and Southeast Asia. The Ecuadorian expedition was led by academy members Louis Godin, Pierre Bouguer, and Charles Marie de La Condamine. With them came seven other Frenchmen, including a doctor-botanist, Godin's cousin, a surgeon, a naval engineer, and a draftsman.

Tensions hampered the expedition from the start, as Bouguer and La Condamine quickly learned they did not get along. Bouguer was stern, stoic, and accused of being paranoid about competitors, while La Condamine, a protégé of Voltaire, was comparatively easygoing. This personal rivalry sparked numerous quarrels as the extroverted, enthusiastic La Condamine effectively assumed leadership of the expedition.

The group arrived in Cartagena, Colombia, in 1735. There they were joined by two Spaniards, both naval captains under secret orders from the king of Spain to report back on the French expedition and conditions in the Spanish territories. In March 1736 the party sailed into Ecuador's Pacific port of Manta and soon traveled via Guayaquil to Quito. Quiteños received the earth measurers with delight, and dances and receptions filled the days following their arrival. As the festivities continued, Pedro Vicente Maldonado, an Ecuadorian mapmaker and mathematician, was chosen to join the historic expedition.

Eventually, the group got down to business. For the sake of accuracy, it was decided that the measurements would be made in the flat plains near Yaruquí, 19 kilometers northeast of Quito. As the work progressed, troubles mounted. The French and Spanish, unused to the elevation and the cold of the Sierra, began to fall ill. Soon the group suffered its first death: the nephew of the academy's treasurer, one of the youngest team members.

As the mourning scientists wandered the plains with their strange instruments, local residents grew suspicious. Rumors began circulating that they had come to dig up and steal buried treasure, maybe

large windows justifies the prices of its restaurant (lunch and dinner daily, entrées $9-12). There's also a smaller café that sells drinks and snacks.

A few hours' hike will bring you to the bottom of the crater and left up the Calacalí road to a very basic hikers refuge, where you can spend the night; the stay is included with your admission to the reserve. Bring your own food, because there aren't any restaurants in the crater, and bring your own bedding. Hike over the rims to rejoin the paved road to Calacalí (10-15 kilometers, 3-4 hours), where you can catch a bus back to the Mitad del Mundo. It's also possible to circle the crater rim on foot. Horseback tours of the crater are available through Astrid Müller's Green Horse Ranch (tel. 9/971-5933, ranch@accessinter.net, www.horseranch.de) in Quito.

Rumicucho Ruins

Often tacked onto the end of tours of the area, the modest pre-Inca Rumicucho Ruins (7:30am-5pm daily, $3 pp) consist of a series even Inca gold. The situation became so tense that La Condamine and a fellow member of the expedition were forced to travel to Lima to obtain the viceroy's support. They finally returned in July 1737 with official papers supporting their story. The measurements continued, and by 1739 the goal of determining the true shape of the earth was in sight. Then disastrous news arrived from the academy: The Lapland expedition had succeeded. The earth was flattened at the poles. The verdict was already in.

As La Condamine tried to keep the expedition from disintegrating, more bad luck struck. The party surgeon, Juan Seniergues, became involved in a dispute over a Cuencan woman and was beaten and stabbed to death at a bullfight in the Plaza de San Sebastián by an angry mob sympathetic to his local rival, the woman's former fiancé. The rest of the group sought refuge in a monastery. In the confusion, the team botanist, Joseph de Jussieu, lost his entire collection of plants—representing five years' work, this loss eventually cost him his sanity as well. The team draftsman was then killed in a fall from a church steeple near Riobamba. La Condamine had to fend off accusations from the Spanish crown that he had insulted Spain by omitting the names of the two Spanish officers from commemorative plaques he had already erected at Oyambaro.

The real equator is found at the Museo de Sitio Intiñan, 300 meters east of Mitad del Mundo.

Finally, in March 1743, the remaining scientists made the last measurements, confirming the Lapland expedition's findings and bringing the expedition to an end. Even though they had come in second, the group's efforts did lay the foundation for the entire modern metric system. Some members decided to stay on in Ecuador—two had already married local women—while others traveled to different South American countries. Most went back to Europe. La Condamine, accompanied by Maldonado, rode a raft down the Amazon for four months to the Atlantic Ocean. From there, the pair sailed to Paris, where they brought the first samples of rubber seen in Europe and were welcomed as heroes. Maldonado died of measles in 1748, while La Condamine enjoyed the high life in Paris until his death in 1774.

In 1936, on the 200th anniversary of the expedition's arrival in Ecuador, the Ecuadorian government built a stone pyramid on the equator at San Antonio de Pichincha in honor of the explorers and their work. This pyramid was eventually replaced by the 30-meter-tall monument that stands today at Mitad del Mundo. Busts along the path leading to the monument commemorate the 10 Frenchmen, two Spaniards, and one Ecuadorian who risked their lives—and sanity—for science.

of rough stone walls and terraces on a small hilltop with a commanding view of the windswept surroundings. To get here, take 13 de Junio (the main drag) northeast from San Antonio de Pichincha, then turn right at the Rumicucho sign. It's quite hard to find, so ask around locally or take a taxi.

THE PICHINCHAS

The twin peaks that give the province its name tower over Quito, dominating the landscape as much as the city's history. It was on the flanks of these volcanoes that Ecuador won its independence in 1822. Both are named Pichincha, which is thought to come from indigenous words meaning "the weeper of good water." **Rucu** (Elder) is actually shorter (4,700 meters) and nearer to the city, while **Guagua** (Baby) stands 4,794 meters high and has always been the more poorly behaved of the two.

Climbing Rucu is easier and more accessible, requiring no special equipment. Unfortunately, the trail to Rucu has been plagued by robberies in recent years. The opening of the *telefériqo* (cable car) has led to increased security, but it is wise to inquire locally about the current situation. Currently there are security patrols on the route from Cruz Loma on the weekend but not during the week.

Guagua sat quiet following an eruption in 1660 until October 1999, when it blew out a huge mushroom cloud of ash that blotted out the sun over Quito for a day and covered the capital in ash. Although things seem to have calmed down, you should still check for the latest update on Guagua, which is officially highly active.

Private transportation—preferably a 4WD vehicle—is almost essential to reach Guagua, the farther peak. The starting point is the pueblo of Lloa, southwest of Quito. A dirt road leaves the main plaza and heads up the valley between the Pichinchas, ending in a shelter maintained by the national civil defense directorate. Park here, pay the entry fee ($1), which goes toward the guardian's salary, and don't leave anything of value in the car. Sleeping space for 10 people costs $6 pp per night, including running water and cooking facilities.

Another hour's hike will bring you from the shelter to the summit. The west-facing crater is pocked by smoking fumaroles, active domes, and collapsed craters. A rocky protrusion called the Cresta del Gallo (Rooster's Crest) separates the old inactive side to the south from the newer active area to the north. Several climbing tour operators in Quito offer this trip.

★ MINDO

Set in a tranquil valley at an ideal elevation of 1,250 meters, surrounded by dense cloud forest teeming with birdlife, this small village has blossomed in recent years into Ecuador's best hub for bird-watchers. More than 470 bird species found in the surrounding forest include toucans, barbets, golden-headed quetzals, and hummingbirds galore, and there are also 250 species of butterflies and 80 species of orchids. Mindo isn't all about watching the

trees, however; you can also fly through them on canopy zip-lines if you want a more action-packed trip.

Almost 21,000 hectares of forest, from tropical rainforest to *páramo,* fall within the Mindo-Nambillo Protected Forest, to the east and south of town. The rushing Mindo, Nambillo, and Cinto Rivers drain the area, and there are several waterfalls near Mindo. It's relatively easy to explore parts of the forest alone, but for a better-quality experience, particularly for bird-watchers, hire a local guide.

Mindo is still a relatively low-key place and retains a village atmosphere with few cars. However, more and more hotels are springing up in town and the surrounding area, and Mindo fills up on the weekend with day-trippers from Quito, so consider coming during the week for a quieter experience.

Recreation and Tours

Mindo is filled with knowledgeable bird-watching guides, who can lead you through the forests at dawn to see toucans and quetzals, and also up to leks, where brilliant crimson-colored Andean cock-of-the-rock males compete for females. Most guides charge small groups $60 for half-day trips and $100 for a full day. Randy Vickers (tel. 2/217-0056) is a bilingual American guide who can arrange extensive bird tours of Mindo and throughout the country. Other recommended guides include Marcela Arias (tel. 9/9340-6321), Julia Patiño (tel. 8/616-2816), and Alex Luna (ayalu_82@hotmail.com). For extended bird-watching tours in Mindo and elsewhere in Ecuador, contact Andean Birding (Salazar Gómez E-1482 and Eloy Alfaro, tel. 2/224-4426, www.andeanbirding.com) in Quito.

The Yellow House (no address, located near the south end of the main park, tel. 2/217-0124, http://ecuadormindobirds.com) is a privately owned 200 hectare reserve covering secondary and primary forest close to town. Bird guides frequent the trails of the reserve for the amazing amount of birds on the property and the cascading views of the

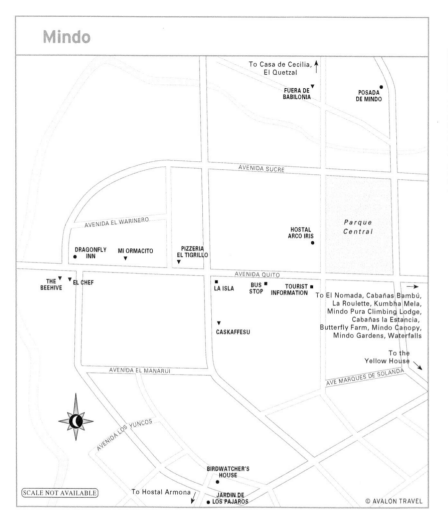

Mindo

To Casa de Cecilia, El Quetzal

FUERA DE BABILONIA

POSADA DE MINDO

AVENIDA SUCRE

AVENIDA EL WARINERO

Parque Central

HOSTAL ARCO IRIS

DRAGONFLY INN   MI ORMACITO

PIZZERIA EL TIGRILLO

AVENIDA QUITO

THE BEEHIVE   EL CHEF

LA ISLA   BUS STOP   TOURIST INFORMATION

To El Nomada, Cabañas Bambú, La Roulette, Kumbha Mela, Mindo Pura Climbing Lodge, Cabañas la Estancia, Butterfly Farm, Mindo Canopy, Mindo Gardens, Waterfalls

CASKAFFESU

To the Yellow House

AVENIDA EL MANARUI

AVE MARQUES DE SOLANDA

AVENIDA LOS YUNCOS

BIRDWATCHER'S HOUSE

SCALE NOT AVAILABLE   To Hostal Armona   JARDIN DE LOS PAJAROS   © AVALON TRAVEL

Mindo valley. A $3 entrance fee is charged to nonguests and maps are provided.

Hostal el Descanso (tel. 2/390-0443), at the far corner of town, is run by a friendly Ecuadorian whose back garden is a haven for many species of hummingbirds. He charges $2 to sit and watch as they fly in and out. To reach Hostal el Descanso, take the first right heading south from the town entrance down an unnamed street, which dead-ends in Lluvia de Oro.

A German-Ecuadorian couple owns a

section of seven hectares of land uphill from Mindo called **Mindo Lindo** (tel. 9/291-5840, www.mindolindo.com), which offers easy access to the cloud forest. They charge $5 pp to use the trails and $25 pp for accommodation.

Southeast of town is the best access point into the **Bosque Protector Mindo-Nambillo** cloudforest. The road leads past several sets of accommodation before splitting. Take the left fork to reach the butterfly farm **Mariposas de Mindo** (www.mariposasdemindo.com, 9am-6:30pm daily,

$5), which breeds 25 species, including the Brown Owl Eye and the Peleides Blue Morpho, the latter with a wingspan of 20cm. The tour follows the lifecycle from eggs to caterpillars to pupae to butterfly. Come in the early morning and you may see them hatch.

Walking up to the right where the road forks takes you to the canopy tour. Mindo Canopy Adventure (tel. 8/542-8758, www.mindocanopy.com) was actually first to bring their expert knowledge of zip-lines from Costa Rica in 2006. The company is fully accredited and has an excellent safety record. A total of 13 lines range up to 400 meters in length and 120 meters in height. You can spend 1.5 hours zipping across all 13 for $20 or do three lines for $10. Try out the "superman" or "butterfly" poses for extra fun. There is also a new *extreme Tarzan swing,* a 40-meter-long pendulum.

If you haven't had your fill of adrenaline kicks, an unusual alternative to rafting is tubing—tumbling down the river rapids in an inflatable tube. This can be arranged with any of the agencies in Mindo ($10 pp).

About one kilometer up the hill from the canopy company is a more relaxed way to travel across the treetops. La Tarabita cable car cruises 150 meters above a river basin and

on the far side there are trails leading to seven waterfalls. Although the paths are not well-marked, you're unlikely to get lost because the route is circular. The entire circuit takes about two hours and gets muddy in places, so bring boots and waterproof clothing as there is regular rainfall. Use of the cable car and entrance to the waterfalls costs $5 pp. There is another waterfall on the opposite side, Tambillo (entrance $5 pp), where you can swim or slide downstream. Walking up to La Tarabita and the waterfalls takes about an hour from town so consider taking a taxi for $7.

Endemic Tours (Av. Quito and Gallo de la Peña, tel. 2/217-0265) rents bicycles for one and a half hour for $5, four hours $10, and all day $15. Take any road out of town and discover the incredible scenery of the cloud forest on two wheels.

A recommended tour operator that can organize all of the activities listed above, including transportation, is La Isla, with an office on the main street (Av. Quito, tel. 2/217-0181, www.laislamindo.com).

About 2km down the road from the Butterfly Farm is Mindo Pura Vida (tel. 9/275-3061, http://mindopuravida.com), the town's newest lodge, which is unique for its

a home in the quaint village of Mindo

climbing wall and slack lines. Belay support is available and there is a small restaurant. The enthusiastic owner plans to build another three-story wall and develop the heavily gardened property.

In town, it's worth heading up to El Quetzal, a hotel north of town on 9 de Octubre, to see how chocolate is made. The price of $5 includes an hour-long explanation of the process and a free brownie, hot chocolate, or ice cream. West of town, Mindo Lago organizes an evening walk to hear a frog chorus (6:30pm daily, $5).

The Bee Hive (tel. 2/217-0296), just over the bridge at the beginning of town, gives those interested an off-beat tour of the owner's beehives starting at the café and venturing out to their property 20 minutes outside of town.

Accommodations

IN MINDO

On the northern edge of town, Casa de Cecilia (north of 9 de Octubre, tel. 2/217-0243, $8 pp) is the best budget option with rooms in two rustic cabins on the edge of a roaring river. On the main Avenida Quito as you arrive in town, The Dragonfly Inn (Quito and Sucre, tel. 2/217-0426, $30 s, $50 d), a wooden cabin-style hotel, is a good mid-range choice with balconies overlooking a garden patio along the river.

El Quetzal (north of 9 de Octubre, tel. 2/217-0034, www.elquetzaldemindo.com, $26 pp including breakfast) has three rooms and lots of chocolate made on the premises. Posada de Mindo (Vicente Aguirre, tel. 2/217-0199; $20 pp) has newer cabins with a good restaurant attached.

Walking southwest of the main street along Colibries are two great-value mid-range options. On the right, Jardín de Los Pajaros (Colibries, tel. 2/217-0159, $15 s, $27 d including breakfast) has comfortable rooms, a balcony lounge, and a small heated pool. Further down, another rustic place adjoining the soccer field is the friendly Hostal Armonia (Colibries, tel. 2/217-0131, $15 pp), which is packed full of orchids and has private cabins with hot water. Nonguests can visit the impressive orchid garden for $2.

VICINITY OF MINDO

Walking east of town towards the reserve, there are plenty of pleasant cabins set in the forest. The first is Cabañas la Estancia (tel. 9/878-3272, www.mindohosterialaestancia. com, $17 pp) with spacious cabins across a rickety bridge set in landscaped gardens with

The Bee Hive is a local travelers' hub.

an outdoor restaurant, a swimming pool, and even a waterslide. Camping is available and costs from $3 pp. Over the bridge and up the hill is Cabañas Bambu (tel. 2/217-0218, dorms $15 pp, cabins from $20 pp) with cabins and rooms nestled in extensive gardens. There's a small restaurant, pool, and hot tub. Halfway to the Butterfly Farm is the Swiss/Ecuadorian-run La Roulotte (tel.8/976-4484, www.la.roulotte.ec, $35 one person, $56 two people). Tastefully decorated gypsy wagons serve as sleeping accommodations surrounding an expansive central dining hall that doubles as a bird-watching station. Toucans and hummingbirds are frequent visitors spotted daily in the peaceful confines of the property.

Past the Butterfly Farm is one of the best options in town, Mindo Gardens (tel. 9/722-3260, www.mindogardens.com, rooms $59-73 s or $81-93 d including breakfast), with comfy, brightly-colored cabins on a 300-hectare private reserve of forest and waterfalls. There's a restaurant right on the Río Mindo and the cabins have private bathrooms with hot water.

Near the Mindo Gardens Lodge, El Monte Sustainable Lodge (tel. 2/217-0102, www.ecuadorcloudforest.com, $96 pp) is run by American Tom Quesenberry and his Ecuadorian wife, Mariela Tenorio. They offer three wood cabins at the edge of the Río Mindo with hot water, private baths, and thatched roofs. Rates include all meals and birding guides for the hiking trails nearby. Cross the river on a small cable car to reach the hotel.

Food

Mindo's small size means that there is only a small group of restaurants to choose from. For budget eats, the main road in town, Avenida Quito, is the place to look. The best here is El Chef (Quito and Colibries, tel. 2/390-0478, 8am-8pm daily, entrées $4-7) where the set lunch is a great value at $2.50 and the specialty is thick, juicy barbecued steak. Also on the main street is Mi Ormacito (Av. Quito, no phone, lunch and dinner daily, entrées $4-5) for seafood. A new café owned by a friendly

and helpful German/Ecuadorian couple, The Bee Hive (8:30am-7pm daily, tel. 217-0296, $3-10), is located across the street from the Dragonfly at the beginning of town. They proudly offer homemade bread and sweets, honey from their beehives, espresso, and light breakfast and lunch fare including smorgasbords. If you catch Ingo, the owner, at the right time, there is also homemade schnapps! Honey, chutney, jams, and Ecuadorian handicrafts are also for sale.

For the best restaurants, venture away from the main street. Try Caskaffesu (Sixto Durán Ballén and Quito, tel. 2/217-0100, 8am-10pm daily, entrées $4-8) for steak, fish, and vegetarian dishes. They also sell coffee from their coffee plantation and have live music weekly. East of the center is the best pizza, pasta, and gnocchi in Mindo, made in front of you in a wood-burning clay oven at El Nómada (Quito, tel. 2/057-1847, noon-9pm daily, entrées $6-9). Up the street from the park and next to the Casa de Cecilia is El Quetzal (9 de Octubre, tel. 9/217-0034, 8am-8pm daily, entrées $7-13), offering a small but well-done menu with stuffed chicken in BBQ chocolate sauce (made from their own chocolate), steak in a coffee sauce, and a passion fruit ceviche. Nightlife during the week is limited to the disco above El Nómada, but on weekends locals and volunteers mingle all night at Happy Moment Bar and Cafe (north end of Parque Central, no phone, 8pm-2am Fri.-Sat., $2-8).

Information

There's a Centro de Información (8:30am-12:30pm, 1:30pm-5pm Wed.-Sun.) on Avenida Quito near the plaza. Ask for a list of members of the local naturalists guide association. Alternatively, Susan, the owner of Caskaffesu (tel. 2/217-0100), or Ingo from The Bee Hive (tel. 2/217-0296) can steer you in the right direction.

Getting There

The road from Quito to Mindo runs west from Mitad del Mundo. It joins the old road just north of Mindo and continues west to

Los Bancos and Puerto Quito. An eight-kilometer road connects Mindo to the main highway. By bus, it's around 2.5 hours from Quito to Mindo. Direct buses from Quito with the Cooperative Flor del Valle leave from the Ofelia terminal at 8am, 9am, 11am, 1pm, and 4pm Monday-Friday; at 7:40am, 8:20am, 9:20am, 11am, 1pm, and 4pm Saturday; and at 7:40am, 8:20am, 9:20am, 2pm, and 5pm Sunday. Quito's Carcelén terminal also has indirect buses to Mindo. Daily buses return from Mindo to Quito at 6:30am, 11am, 1:45pm, 3pm, and 5pm Monday-Friday; 6:30am, 1pm, 2pm, 3:30pm, and 5pm Saturday, and 3pm and 4pm Sunday. The bus station is located in the center of town a block before the main square.

If you miss the bus from Ofelia, take a taxi to Carcelén terminal and take the first bus to Los Bancos, which leaves you on the main road at the top of the hill above Mindo, where you can catch a taxi (from $1). Leaving Mindo, take a taxi to the main road and flag down any Quito-bound bus.

MAQUIPUCUNA BIOLOGICAL RESERVE

More than 4,500 rugged hectares purchased by the Nature Conservancy in 1988 protect the Maquipucuna Biological Reserve ($10 pp), one of the last remaining chunks of cloud forest in northwestern Ecuador. Most of this privately owned and managed reserve is undisturbed primary forest, ranging from a low-elevation (1,200 meters) subtropical zone to cloud forest at the base of 2,800-meter Cerro Montecristi. It's less than three hours from Quito and surrounded by another 14,000 hectares of protected forest.

Temperatures vary from 14-24°C, allowing thousands of plant species to thrive in a wide range of climates. More than 330 species of birds include the cock-of-the-rock and the empress brilliant hummingbird. The reserve is also the first place where spectacled bears have been reintroduced into the wild. Wander farther afield and chances are you'll stumble across a burial mound or a *culunco*—a half

trail, half tunnel between the Andes and the Oriente—left by the pre-Inca Yumbo people.

Next to the open-air Thomas Davis Ecotourism Center at 1,200 meters, the reserve has 10 guest rooms ($83-100 s, $108-134 d per night, three meals included) with shared or private baths.

To get to the reserve, take a bus from Quito's Ofelia station to Nanegal, the nearest village to Maquipucuna. From Nanegal, you'll have to hire a truck or taxi ($10) to take you to Marianitas, which is four kilometers from the reserve entrance.

For more information, contact the Fundación Maquipucuna in Quito (Baquerizo Moreno 238 y Tamayo, tel. 2/250-7200, www.maqui.org).

YANACOCHA

The old Nono-Mindo road offers great birding along almost its entire length. One particularly good spot is Yanacocha, a 964-hectare reserve of elfin *Polylepis* forest in the Pichincha foothills, which protects wildlife from agricultural expansion in the region. Take a turnoff to the left (south) 18 kilometers from Quito and drive up to the gate. The $5 pp entry fee helps the Fundación Jocotoco (www.fjocotoco.org) protect special bird areas around Ecuador. Twenty-two species of hummingbirds have been spotted in the vicinity, including the endangered black-breasted pufleg, which lives only in this region and has recently been adopted as the emblem of Quito.

TANDAYAPA LODGE

Iain Campbell, a geology expert turned birding guide, runs this luxury birder lodge along the old Nono-Mindo road. He bills Tandayapa (Reina Victoria 1684 and La Pinta, Ed. Santiago 1, Dep. 501, tel./fax 2/244-7520, www.tandayapa.com, $148 s, $248 d, all meals included) as "the only lodge in the world designed by birders, owned by birders, and run for birders by birders." You can tell it's the real thing: 4am breakfasts are no problem, and they've already planted 30,000 trees in the immediate area to help combat deforestation.

The 12 guestrooms all have private baths with hot water. They're in a single building with a fireplace, bar, and a balcony overlooking the cloud forest, making it easy to start your day with new sightings. They've seen 18 species of hummingbirds from the balcony feeders alone, and a total of 320 species of birds on their trails. Many species are "staked out," meaning the guides know where they are on a regular basis. Packages including guides and transportation are available. Three-, four-, and five-day packages are available.

To reach Tandayapa, either head up the old Nono-Mindo road (now called the *Ecoruta Paseo del Quindé*) or take the new road and get off the bus at the turnoff at Km 52. It's seven kilometers to the lodge from there (11 kilometers from Nanegalito). Alternatively, private transportation from Quito is available for 1-5 people for $115; a small bus for up to 12 people costs $135. The lodge also offers cars with drivers for day trips for $135 (1-3 people), $150 (4-5 people), and $170 (up to 12 people).

BELLAVISTA CLOUD FOREST RESERVE

British ecologist and teacher Richard Parsons began with 55 hectares of prime cloud forest near the town of Tandayapa in 1991, where he built a four-story thatched-roof lodge looking out over the moss-covered treetops. Interested ornithologists and friends have helped increase the size of the reserve to 700 hectares, and three comfortable houses plus a research station for students and scientists have all been added. Bellavista Cloud Forest Reserve includes four waterfalls and 10 kilometers of trails along which birders can search through the premontane cloud forest (1,400-2,600 meters) for the tanager finch, giant antpitta, and white-faced nunbird that frequent nearby streams.

Private rooms ($120.78 s, $102.48 d, with all meals; $77 s, $103 d without) are available in the original geodesic dome buildings, and upstairs are dorms ($66 pp with meals, $33 pp without). For more privacy, choose one of the three newer houses for the same prices.

Campsites ($6 pp) and hostel-style lodging in the research station ($19 pp per night) are available. Day trips from Quito ($120 s, $99 d) include guides, transportation, and two meals, and two- and three-day packages are also possible. Arrange visits through the reserve's office in Quito (Jorge Washington E7-23 and 6 de Diciembre, tel./fax 2/223-2313, www.bellavistacloudforest.com).

Transportation can be arranged from Quito, or take a public bus to Nanegalito from the terminal at Ofelia. Any bus to Pacto, Puerto Quito, San Miguel de los Bancos, or Mindo passes Nanegalito. Ask in Nanegalito about renting a pickup truck ($15) to travel the last 15 kilometers to the reserve. If you're driving yourself, head for Mitad del Mundo and Calacalí on the new road to Esmeraldas, and turn left at Km 52, just across a bridge (look for the "Bellavista" sign). Follow this road six kilometers to the village of Tandayapa, then uphill another six kilometers to the reserve. You can also continue on the road to Esmeraldas through the town of Nanegalito to Km 62, then turn left and follow signs along the ridge for 12 kilometers to Bellavista. The third access is at Km 77, just one kilometer from the Mindo entrance; then drive the 12 kilometers of unpaved road to the reserve.

HOSTERÍA SAN JORGE

Four kilometers up the road from Cotocollao to Nono in a 93-hectare mountain reserve is Hostería San Jorge (Vía Antigua a Nono Km. 4, tel. 2/224-7549, www.hostsanjorge. com.ec, $77 s, $85 d), run by the friendly and enthusiastic George Cruz. The traditional country house, once owned by former Ecuadorian president Eloy Alfaro, offers wonderful views of the Quito valley from 3,000 meters up the Pichincha foothills. Gardens, a lake, and a spring-fed swimming pool and hot tub surround the guest rooms warmed by fireplaces on chilly evenings. It is a good place to acclimate, and the owners offer a wealth of activities, including birding in the backyard and treks on pre-Inca trails to the coast. The Mindo and Nono areas are within mountain-biking distance. You can get here by taxi or call for pickup.

SANGOLQUÍ

Corn is king in the town of Sangolquí, southeast of Quito. A 10-meter statue of a cob, called "El Choclo," greets visitors in a traffic circle at the entrance. In late June, festivities mark the end of the harvest. During the fourth and final day, bullfights become venues for raging displays of machismo as alcohol-numbed locals try to get as close to the bull as possible without getting killed—unsurprisingly, someone usually gets injured. The central plaza area has been beautifully restored, and the town hosts an excellent indigenous market on Sundays and a smaller one on Thursdays. To get here, take a "Sangolquí" bus from the local terminal at Marin Bajo.

PASOCHOA PROTECTED FOREST

The densest, most unspoiled stretch of forest close to Quito is the Pasochoa Protected Forest (open daily, $5 pp), 30 kilometers southeast of the city. A long sloping valley preserves the original lush wooded state of the area surrounding Quito. The reserve ranges 2,700-4,200 meters in elevation, the highest point being Cerro Pasochoa, an extinct volcano. Primary and secondary forest topped by *páramo* supports 126 species of birds, including many hummingbirds and a family of condors.

Loop paths of varying lengths and difficulty lead higher and higher into the hills, ranging 2-8 hours in length. It's also possible to climb to the lip of Cerro Pasochoa's blasted volcanic crater in six hours. Campsites and a few dorm rooms with showers and cooking facilities are available near the bottom. Free guided tours are sometimes available.

From Quito, take a bus marked "Playón" from the south end of the Plaza La Marín below Old Town to the village of Amaguaña (30-40 minutes, $0.60). Hire a pickup ($5-8) from the plaza in Amaguaña to the turnoff for the reserve, which is marked by a green sign facing south one kilometer toward Machachi on the Panamericana. From there, a dirt road leads seven kilometers up a rough, cobbled road to the reserve. Drivers may agree to come back for you, or you could catch a ride down with the reserve personnel in the evening. Take a phone card, and you can call from the cell phone at the entrance for a taxi to pick you up.

Some tour operators in Quito offer group day trips to Pasochoa.

Photo Credits

About the Author

Ben Westwood

Ben Westwood dreamed of being a writer and musician from an early age. Growing up in England, he combined the two by studying music and getting involved in student journalism in London. He wrote his first travel journal during a backpacking trip through Southeast Asia.

After graduating from college, Ben decided to follow his passion for travel; with an English-language teaching qualification under his belt, he set off for Ecuador. In the year he spent there, he fell in love with the country – and one of its citizens. He returned to the UK, newly married, to complete a postgraduate degree at the country's top journalism school, City University.

Ben worked for *The Daily Telegraph* and Telegraph.co.uk as a travel journalist and online travel editor, writing articles on everything from encounters with Maoist guerrillas in Nepal to encounters with drunken Brits in Greece. After a brief stint working in adventure tourism, Ben moved to Ecuador to combine his passions for teaching and travel writing. In addition to *Moon Ecuador & the Galápagos Islands*, he is the author of *Moon Machu Picchu* and *Moon Peru*. He has also contributed to the *The Rough Guide to South America on a Budget*, *The Daily Telegraph*, *The Independent*, and *The Guardian*.

Ben currently teaches journalism and tourism at Brighton University in the UK. He still finds time to sing and play the guitar, and has released one self-funded album, *Keep Dreaming*. Follow him on Twitter @BenWestwood and at soundcloud.com/benwestwoodmusic.

About the Contributor

Jon Jared first experienced the itch for travel during summer trips with his grandparents to England, Scotland, and Wales. After visiting Zambia and traversing the mountain towns of Colorado, he moved to Ecuador in 2007 in search of a new understanding of the world around him.

In Ecuador, Jon has worked at hotels, restaurants, and bars; served as a local guide, a freelance writer, and editor; and managed the South American Explorers Club in Quito, where he currently lives.

MOON SPOTLIGHT QUITO
Avalon Travel
a member of the Perseus Books Group
1700 Fourth Street
Berkeley, CA 94710, USA
www.moon.com

Editor: Nikki Ioakimedes
Series Manager: Kathryn Ettinger
Contributor: Jon Jared
Copy Editor: Kim Runciman
Graphics and Production Coordinator:
  Lucie Ericksen
Map Editor: Mike Morgenfeld
Cartographer: Stephanie Poulain

ISBN-13: 978-1-63121-035-8

Text © 2014 by Ben Westwood and
  Avalon Travel.
Maps © 2014 by Avalon Travel.
All rights reserved.

Front cover photo: People at the Church of
  San Francisco in Quito © powerofforever/
  Istockphoto.com

Printed in the United States

All recommendations, including those for sights,
activities, hotels, restaurants, and shops, are
based on each author's individual judgment.
We do not accept payment for inclusion in our
travel guides, and our authors don't accept
free goods or services in exchange for positive
coverage.

Although every effort was made to ensure
that the information was correct at the time of
going to press, the author and publisher do not
assume and hereby disclaim any liability to any
party for any loss or damage caused by errors,
omissions, or any potential travel disruption
due to labor or financial difficulty, whether
such errors or omissions result from negligence,
accident, or any other cause.

Keeping Current

If you have a favorite gem you'd like to see included in the next edition, or see anything
that needs updating, clarification, or correction, please drop us a line. Send your
comments via email to feedback@moon.com, or use the address above.